Welcome

MW00903589

The Fellowship for Intentional Community is pleased to offer you the cream of our crop—the very best articles that have appeared over the last 20 years in our flagship publications: *Communities* magazine and *Communities Directory*. We've distilled what we consider the most insightful and helpful articles on the topics that you—our readers—have told us you care about most, and have organized them into 15 scintillating collections:

I.   **Intentional Community Overview; Starting a Community**
II.   **Seeking and Visiting a Community**
III. **Leadership, Power, and Membership**
IV.   **Good Meetings**
V.   **Consensus**
VI.   **Agreements, Conflict, and Communication**
VII. **Relationships, Intimacy, Health, and Well-Being**
VIII. **Children in Community**
IX.   **Community for Elders**
X.   **Sustainable Food, Energy, and Transportation**
XI.   **Green Building, Ecovillage Design, and Land Preservation**
XII. **Cohousing**
XIII. **Cooperative Economics and Creating Community Where You Are**
XIV. **Challenges and Lessons of Community**
XV.   **The Peripatetic Communitarian: The Best of Geoph Kozeny**

On average, each collection is comprised of 15–20 articles, containing a total of 55–65 pages. All are available both as downloadable PDFs and as print copies. Buy one, buy several, or buy the whole set! While there's a smattering of classic pieces that date back to the '90s, the vast majority of these offerings have been written in the past dozen years, representing cutting-edge thinking and how-to explorations of the social, ecological, and economic aspects of sustainable living. We've gathered insights about what you can expect when raising children in community, and offer a wealth of information about what it's like to grow old there, too. For dessert, we have the collected wisdom of over 50 essays from Geoph Kozeny (1949–2007), the Peripatetic Communitarian.

If you're hungry for information about cooperative living, we have a menu that will satisfy any appetite! If you're thinking about starting a community, this collection offers an incredible storehouse of practical advice. If you're thinking of joining a community, our packets will help you discern the right things to look for, and how to be a savvy shopper. If you're just curious about community and want to snack, our smörgåsbord of tasty nuggets will let you pick and choose what's most appealing.

Bon appétit!

Laird Schaub
FIC Executive Secretary
November 2013

Cooperative Economics and Creating Community Where You Are

On the three-legged stool of sustainability, less attention has been given to economics than to the more robust ecological and social dimensions. But that doesn't mean it's less important. (It's hard to keep a stool upright with only two legs.) Half the articles in this bundle are focused on what we're learning about values-based ways to make a living (which is a quality of life issue if there ever was one).

The other stories are devoted to taking the inspiration of community beyond the boundary of shared property. If you figure that there are only 100,000 people in the US living in some form of self-identified intentional community, yet 100 *million* wanting a greater sense of community in their life, it's obvious that we should be exporting what we're learning to neighborhoods, churches, schools, and workplaces almost everywhere. Half of the 20 articles in this bundle focus on that expansive task.

—*Laird Schaub. FIC Executive Secretary, November 2013*

Craig Gibson can see many of his community investments from his garden at Findhorn.

RECIPE FOR A THRIVING COMMUNITY

BY JONATHAN DAWSON

- *Keep your money in the community.*

- *Circulate it through as many hands as possible.*

- *Earn it, spend it, and invest it in member-owned retail and service businesses.*

- *Save it in home-grown financial institutions.*

- *Enjoy.*

THE VIEW FROM CRAIG GIBSON'S WILD AND ABUNDANT PERMA-culture garden at the Findhorn Foundation in northern Scotland is deeply familiar and reassuring. On one side towers Moya, the community's wind turbine, in which Craig is an investor and shareholder. On the other side is Dunelands, a member-owned woodlot cooperative, of which Craig is a member, that manages and coppices the community's woodland. Also within view is the collection point for Earth Share CSA Farm (community-supported agriculture), where every Friday almost 200 subscribers collect boxes of fresh organic vegetables. Craig was also one of the initial investors in the "Cowshare" plan, established by another community member as a way of raising investment capital within the community to buy dairy cows. Craig gets his dividends in cheese and in manure for his garden.

1

From his garden he can also see the community bank, Ekopia Exchange, which enables community members like him to invest in community businesses. Next door to Ekopia is the Phoenix, a shop in which Craig is also a shareholder, which has benefited from loans provided by Ekopia Exchange. In the Phoenix, as in most of the other businesses within the community—the Foundation (which runs educational courses), the café, the bakery, the theatre, the building company, the IT services company, and the many self-employed artisans, therapists and artists—people pay for goods and services not only with the British pound sterling, but with the "EKO," the community's own currency.

You might suppose that Craig, a musician and builder, is a rich man—an investor in half a dozen companies all of which he can survey from his own proud estate. Hardly!

"How I've managed to find the various bits of cash that make up these investments, I just couldn't tell you," he reflects with genuine surprise. "In part, it's because these community businesses made it easy, allowing payments over

FINDHORN AS ECOVILLAGE

I define "ecovillage" as the intention to explore a way to tread more lightly and with more happiness on the Earth. It relates to how we grow our food, build our houses, recycle our waste, generate our power, make our decisions, work with our conflicts, and develop relationships with other species and with spirit. —J.D.

time. But also in large part, it's just a matter of priorities. It is really important that we nurture what we have created here at Findhorn and use whatever resources we can muster to support its economy—and not guns and bombs and cigarettes or whatever else mainstream banks would invest our savings in."

This seems to be the nub of what allows Craig and others living in ecovillages like Findhorn to practice some form of right livelihood. "What is critically important is for a community to start putting all the pieces together in one place," writes Michael Shuman in *Going Local.* "Then, and only then, can you begin to enjoy the synergies that occur when local ownership is linked with local production, local investing, local purchasing, and local employment."

The synergies are critical here. Membership in a CSA farm, for example, is clearly a very good thing. However, while it improves the nutritional quality of your food and allows you to reduce the miles you drive to buy it, being a CSA member makes a significant difference in only one area of your life. So many of the other patently unjust, unsustainable, and unsatisfying dimensions of modern life—the need to make money in jobs that serve neither the self nor the planet, the commuting required to get to work, the energy-intensive nature of most human settlements and dwellings, the conditions under which most of our clothing, furniture, and other pos-

FINDHORN'S VILLAGE ECONOMY

BY DAVID HOYLE

FINDHORN'S COMMUNITY ECONOMY IS ONE OF THE MOST DEVELOPED of any ecovillage worldwide, with an annual income in excess of $8 million and an asset base of over $10 million. Collectively it employs over 200 people in approximately 45 businesses and organisations, along with a number of self-employed therapists, artists, and craftspeople.

The primary income-producing activities at Findhorn are personal development courses, overnight accommodations, ecological building, retail, organic agriculture, publishing, printing, and generating renewable energy.

Currently about a third of community residents are employed as staff of the Findhorn Foundation, a nonprofit educational organization. Its employees work in administration or host workshops in exchange for food, accommodations, and a monthly allowance. Most other Findhorn residents are employed by member-owned businesses or are self-employed.

The Findhorn economy is served by several on-site or regional financial institutions:

• EKO Currency System, a community-wide local currency.
• Ekopia Resource Exchange: A community economic co-operative (like a small-scale community investment bank) with over 200 members and investment capital in excess of $600,000. Ekopia administers the EKO Currency System.
• Two local LETS systems. (LETS is a reciprocal-credit or mutual-trade system that uses a computerized bookkeeping method, rather than a local currency, to keep track of transactions.)
• The satellite branch of a local area credit union.
Primary businesses in the community economy include:
• Findhorn Foundation: A renowned educational centre offering workshops on personal development, spirituality, and sustainability.
• New Findhorn Directions, Ltd.: The business arm of Findhorn Foundation, providing accommodations for guests in the Caravan Park.
• IT Support and Services: Administers and maintains the

David Hoyle is director of Phoenix Community Stores and founder of its Ekopia Resource Exchange.

Money is to the community as blood is to the body—a circulating substance that provides nourishment to every community member through whose hands it passes.

sessions are made, and on and on—all too often remain beyond our control. We live in a world where it is damned hard for good people to live rightly and lightly. The forces ranged against wise and skillful action often seem just too great to fight against.

But put the various pieces of the economic picture *together*—combining locally-based investment, consumption, ownership, and employment—and it becomes much more possible to re-weave the web of community and right liveli-

hood. Take the money system, for example. Money is to the community as blood is to the body—a circulating substance that benefits and provides nourishment to every person through whose hands it passes as it moves through the community. In

roads and other physical infrastructure of The Park, the community's primary property.

• Phoenix Community Stores: One of the UK's leading alternative retail outlets, comprised of speciality shops including the Food Market, Bakery, Café, Bookstore, Apothecary, and Craft and Gift Centre. The Phoenix rents its various premises from the Findhorn Foundation; however, it's hoped that one day investors will be able to purchase its land and buildings as well.

• Findhorn Flower Essences: Producers of flower essence products and workshops on flower essences.

• Aromantic: A retail business offering a range of essential oils and workshops.

• Earth Share: A leading CSA farm with over 200 member/shareholders.

• Wester Lawrenceton Farm: An award-winning organic dairy farm producing cheese and eggs for the community and for shops throughout the UK.

• Dunelands Woodlot Cooperative.

• Moya Wind Turbine Cooperative.

• Post House Printing: A full-service printer and graphic design service.

• Findhorn Press: A successful book publisher.

• Steiner School: A school offering Rudolf Steiner-based education from kindergarten to age 14.

• Universal Hall: A 350-seat community arts centre that produces its own events and rents out facilities for local, national, and international productions.

• Eco-Village Limited: An ecological design, development, and construction company.

• Build One: An ecological building co-operative.

• Eco-Village Training: An educational organization offering courses and workshops on ecovillage living and development.

• Trees for Life: An educational charity focusing on ecological reforestation. Ω

For more information: www. findhorn.org

For the last 30 years David Hoyle has worked in the natural foods movement in the UK, Europe, Canada, and the U.S., and for the last 12 years as Director of Phoenix Community Stores at Findhorn, and as founder of its Ekopia Resource Exchange.

Many Findhorn residents earn a living on site.

a worst-case scenario, money entering a community leaves almost immediately because residents must spend it elsewhere for basic necessities like water, food, shelter, gas, electric energy, clothing, and so on. Up to 80 percent of the money coming into many American Indian reservations, for example, is spent outside the reservation within 48 hours. Consider the math. If $100 comes into the system, after one spending cycle only $20 remains, after two cycles just $4, then just $1—yielding a total value to the community as it circulates of just $125. But reverse the equation

community. Here, the synergies become apparent. Many of the goods for sale in the Phoenix community shop could be purchased more cheaply at the supermarket in town. However, for those with services to sell within the community (which, if you think about it, is just about everyone: baby-sitting, jam-making, potted plants, massage, construction skills, and so on), it makes sense to buy within the community because that creates a demand for the goods and services that residents want to sell.

Moreover, shareholders in the Phoenix shop earn a five percent discount on all purchases made there, and they get to watch the value of their investment grow as the shop prospers. As it grows, so employment increases, more money stays in the system, and everyone gains.

Or take the less visible benefits of sharing ownership in our various businesses. Membership in the CSA farm requires not just a financial payment but also three work shifts over the course of a season. Three workshifts times 200 subscribers

Folks like Craig work long hours for relatively modest financial returns. But the rewards come increasingly from achievements other than simply collecting money in the bank. They come from the view of the wind turbine generating our power, from the employment being created for our young people, from access to a growing number of goods produced without exploiting people or the planet, from the joys of being active participants rather than passive consumers in our community economy.

People visiting Findhorn are often struck by how much singing, dancing, and sharing goes on here, and how important these are in creating a feeling of well-being within the community. Less visible, but no less important, is getting the economy right, so a high proportion of members can work within the community, engaged in a way that feels meaningful and of value to self, the community, and the planet.

Meanwhile, back in Craig's garden, the feeling of well-being is tangible. Here there is no waste: anything biodegradable that's gone missing from elsewhere in the community has likely found its way into the garden, the compost heap, a new garden shed, or the new addition to Craig's house (of which 75 percent of the materials are recycled). At the foot of the hill, new natural-built, sustainable dwellings emerge in the five-acre meadow known as the Field of Dreams. A steady stream of friends and students pass through the Foundation's many educational programmes, helping with the fruit harvest and catching a glimpse of how society might be differently ordered. The great learning—about how we can live on the Earth with more insight and compassion—takes one small but tangible step forward. Ω

"[It] is critically important for a community to start putting all the pieces together in one place. Then, and only then, can you begin to enjoy the synergies that occur when local ownership is linked with local production, local investing, local purchasing, and local employment." —Michael Shuman

so that only 20 percent of the $100 leaves the system on each spending cycle, and the total value to the community is around $500 as the original $100 circulates.

Why not go still further and create a closed economic system, where 100 percent of incoming money is retained in the community? In 2002, the first year the Findhorn Foundation issued its EKO currency, the 10,000 EKOs put into circulation are estimated to have generated a turnover resulting in a value of in excess of $225,000 during the year (i.e., 2002). A significant amount of this value, if it was pounds sterling instead of EKOs, would otherwise have been spent outside the

equals a lot of work parties, a lot of reconnection with other community members and with the land, and a lot of community ownership of the project. And when the CSA farm has a hard year, there's a plentiful supply of willing labour to call on.

A different ethic emerges. Sure, one could draw larger dividends from a conventional stock market investment; earn a higher salary from regular, mainstream employment; buy butter and jam more cheaply at the supermarket. But a shift is taking place, a redefinition of values, a choice for ownership of and commitment to a community that's beginning to take control of its own economic health and destiny.

Jonathan Dawson, Executive Secretary of GEN-Europe (the Global Ecovillage Network), lives at Findhorn Foundation Community where he teaches Right Livelihood through the annual ecovillage training programme. For more information: jonathan@gen-europe.org.

Note: We retain the spelling of our British authors.

Regaining Our Sense of Oneness through Localization

By Helena Norberg-Hodge

A central theme in most spiritual traditions is oneness—a sense of the inextricable interdependence of all life. Most religions speak of our connection with others and the larger cosmos, encouraging us to cultivate an expanded sense of self. From Thich Nhat Hanh, Zen Buddhist monk: "'To be' is to inter-be. We cannot just be by ourselves alone. We have to inter-be with every other thing." From Black Elk, Lakota Holy man: "The first peace, which is the most important, is that which comes from within the souls of men when they realize their relationship, their oneness, with the universe and all its powers."

I have personally experienced the profound influence of these teachings in Ladakh or "Little Tibet," where I have spent much of my time over the last 35 years. There, I experienced first-hand how Buddhism influenced every aspect of traditional life. The Ladakhis possessed an irrepressible joie de vivre. It was impossible to spend any time at all in Ladakh without being won over by their contagious laughter. Of course they had sorrows and problems, and they felt sad when faced with illness or death. Yet the Ladakhis seemed to possess an extended, inclusive sense of self. They did not retreat behind boundaries of fear and self-protection; in fact, they seemed to be totally lacking in what we would call pride. This didn't mean a lack of self-respect. On the contrary, their self-respect was so deep-rooted as to be unquestioned.

Over the years I came to realise that the Ladakhis' joy and dignity was not due to their spiritual beliefs alone, but arose from a subtle and complex interplay between shared community bonds, local economic interactions, and religious practice. Strong communities were built upon economic ties that fostered a daily experience of interdependence. This, in turn, provided a healthy foundation for individuals to grow and be nurtured, to feel that they belonged—to a people, a culture, and their place on earth. This expanded sense of self was further nourished and reinforced by their spiritual beliefs and practices.

In modern consumer society, our connections to each other and to the rest of nature have been largely severed. Almost all our interactions are mediated by large bureaucracies or businesses. In this way, we become dependent on institutions rather than one another. For example, the majority of us are separated from the source of our food by many middle men and hundreds, if not thousands, of miles.

The language of connection has even been co-opted by proponents of economic globalization. For instance, the current slogan of a prominent multinational telecommunications corporation: "We're better, connected." Now, connecting with loved ones means talking on your mobile phone; feeling part of a community is having a profile on Facebook; we don't need to know our neighbours because now we live in a "global village." Sadly, reliance on technologies to connect with others can actually create a sense of separation.

It is this same separation that is behind many of our biggest environmental problems. Our daily lives seem to depend more on a man-made world—the economy, electric power, cars, high-tech medicine—than the natural life support systems of the planet. As we become more separated from the natural world, it becomes increasingly difficult for us to know the effects of our actions on nature or on other people. The ever-expanding scope and scale of the global economy obscures the consequences of our actions: in effect, our arms have been so lengthened that we no longer see what our hands are doing.

5

The scale of the modern nation-state has become so large that leaders would be unable to act according to the principles of interdependence, even if they wished to. When political decisions have global consequences, as they do today, it is nearly impossible for leaders to truly appreciate the full effects of their actions. Decisions are instead made according to abstract economic principles—in the name of "progress"—often disregarding the implications for individual members of society and for the rest of the living world.

In Ladakh, despite thousands of years of Buddhist practice and strong communities, the global economy has nearly severed the connections between people and to the natural world. In the mid-1970s, the region was opened up to "economic development" and submerged in an avalanche of imported consumer goods, tourism, westernised schooling, new polluting technologies—including DDT and asbestos—and

Local economies and close-knit communities are essential for raising healthy people—in body and mind.

development propaganda. Within a decade, poverty and pollution were commonplace. Community bonds had been eroded as people competed for scarce jobs in the new money economy, leading eventually to outright violent conflict. Buddhists and Muslims, who had lived together peacefully for generations, were literally killing each other. Despite their strong spiritual foundations, the Ladakhis were not immune to the pressures of the global economy.

For me the main lesson from Ladakh is the fundamental importance of strengthening local economies in order to maintain or rebuild our real community ties and deep connection to the natural world. Now in the West, we are beginning to rediscover the importance of community in helping us to reconnect with each other and other living beings. Local economies and close-knit communities are also essential for raising healthy people—in body and mind. Universally, research confirms that feeling connected to others and to nature is a fundamental human need. Recent childhood development research demonstrates the importance, in the early years of life, of learning about who we are in relation to parents, siblings, and the larger community. These are *real* role models, unlike the artificial stereotypes found in the media. Communities also provide a supportive framework for our spiritual development. However, without the right economic underpinnings these communities are destined to struggle and ultimately break down. Turning away from globalization and toward the local would create the economic foundations necessary to support local communities on a global scale—an "Economics of Happiness." Through *localization* we could meet our needs, both material and psychological, without compromising the survival of life on earth.

Global collaboration is essential for rebuilding local economies. Sharing experiences with people from other cultures enables us all to make more informed choices of how to construct our communities and economies. Over the last 30 years my organisation, the International Society for Ecology and Culture, has worked with Ladakhi leaders to communicate the on-the-ground realities of life in the West. Our educational campaigns provide Ladakhis with a fuller picture of life in a consumer culture, including the negative sides not shown by the romanticized images in the media. We also demonstrate the numerous positive trends and initiatives that are rebuilding the kind of sustainable culture the Ladakhis have been encouraged to leave behind.

As community-builders, it is vitally important that we reach out to people in developing countries. As globalized economic development sweeps across the planet, people are made to feel primitive and backward. From schoolbooks to blaring television commercials, the message is that more traditional, indigenous ways of life are inferior. Westerners have an important role to play in countering these messages, by showing how we are seeking to regain the connectedness that they have not yet completely lost.

The trajectory of the global economy is not evolutionary; it is not an inevitable process towards a "more developed" individualistic consciousness. It is, in fact, a direct result of policy choices that have favoured multinational corporations over small business, centralization of power over direct democracy, and the accumulation of wealth by the few at the expense of the many. We are free to make other choices. To rekindle the sense of oneness encouraged by our spiritual traditions, we would do well to shift direction—towards localised economic systems that foster connection and care, towards an economics of happiness. ✍

Author and filmmaker Helena Norberg-Hodge is a pioneer of the "new economy" movement. Through writing and public lectures on three continents, she has been promoting an economics of personal, social, and ecological well-being for more than 30 years. Helena's book, Ancient Futures, *together with the film of the same title, has been translated into more than 40 languages, and sold about half a million copies. She is also the producer of the award-winning film,* The Economics of Happiness, *and the co-author of* Bringing the Food Economy Home *and* From the Ground Up: Rethinking Industrial Agriculture. *Helena is director of the International Society for Ecology and Culture (ISEC), a founding member of the International Commission on the Future of Food and Agriculture, and a co-founder of both the International Forum on Globalization and the Global Ecovillage Network.*

BY ALBERT BATES

Members of Dancing Rabbit Ecovillage use their own local currency to buy goods and services from each other.

Our Own Money:
A Recipe for Local Economic Revival

As local groups and communities created their own local scrip currencies and exchange systems, they learned about economists' deepest secret: money and information are equivalent — and neither is scarce!

—Hazel Henderson

In the 1970s, while visiting a cousin who was chasing a degree at Harvard Business School, I learned something about economics that has stayed with me ever since. As my cousin carefully watered his tiny garden, he explained "standard of living" to me. Standard of living is not the product of how well you extract resources or exploit labor, or even how much material wealth you amass, he said. Aristotle long ago warned us that human desires always expand faster than natural resources, and if you try to get ahead in that contest, you will lose.

Standard of living, my cousin explained, as he pruned some brown and yellow leaves from his plants, is a function of the speed at which money bounces back and forth in your economy. It is velocity, not volume, that determines how well off you are.

A little over a decade after that educational foray into Harvard Yard, I came across one of the seminal books for 21st century survival. In *Interest and Inflation Free Money: Creating an Exchange Medium that Works for Everybody and Protects the Earth,* Margrit Kennedy challenged the whole idea that we have to have a money system based on constant growth. Nothing grows endlessly. Nature is a wave. If we have a large expansion, we need a large contraction to balance it. If we are talking about global economies, these large contractions can be seriously damaging. So Kennedy came up with some ideas for economies that are steady state. (See "How a Steady State Economy Could Change our Lives" pg. 42.) Steady state economies don't use interest. They are simply based on the fair exchange of value for value.

If you have your life savings in a bank, Kennedy said, they're probably not going to do you as much good as they would if you invested them in preparing your children to have greater self-reliance or helping one of your neighbors start a business. If you invest in a bank, chances are the money is actually leaving your community entirely. If you invest in your neighborhood, your community, and your region, you are keeping the money at home, where it has nothing to do but speed up its passing from hand to hand.

Kennedy also observed the waxing and waning of local currencies, which tend to proliferate whenever a community perceives a need to protect its internal economy from outside disturbances such as war or depression, or when the national currency collapses and people are forced to devise their own alternatives. Local currencies decline less often from lack of success and more often by government edict, which happens when they are perceived (correctly) as a threat to national banks and the central command and control hierarchy that regulates monetary systems.

In a case study that illustrated my cousin's lesson perfectly, Professor Kennedy went back to the global recession of 1932, to the small Austrian town of Wörgl. Confronted with the collapse of the national currency, the town elders of Wörgl issued 32,000 "Free Schillings" (interest-free Schillings) protected by a deposit of normal Austrian Schillings in a local bank. The clever burgermeisters of Wörgl put a "rest fee" on the normal Austrian Schillings that amounted to one percent per month. The fee had to be paid by the person who held a Free Schilling at the end of the month, and a tax stamp was then glued to it. Without the current stamp, the Free Schilling was worthless. This caused everyone who received a Free Schilling to spend it before they spent their standard Austrian Schillings so they would not have to pay the fees at the end of the month. This meant they spent their Free Schillings first, and they spent them fast. It was a game of musical chairs, and at the end of each month the music sped up, people spent Free Schillings like crazy, and the Wörgl economy boomed.

I imagine everyone just took off work and kicked back for a few days at the start of the month, exhausted from their revelries in the days before.

While ordinary Schillings circulated an average 21 times in the course of a year, Free Schillings circulated 463 times over the same year, and created goods and services worth 14,816,000 Schillings. While most of the countries in Europe suffered dire shortages (setting the stage for ethnic persecution, extreme nation-

JACOB STEVENS

Money is a measurement, not a thing. It is an agreement between people to use something common for all exchanges.

Findhorn member David Hoyle, who founded the community's Ekopia Resource Exchange, holds Ekos, the community currency.

In reality, money is a measurement, not a thing. It is an agreement between people to use something common for all exchanges. For most people, this agreement has been in place since before they were born and is taken for granted. Sometimes, they grow so attached to it that they will staunchly defend it even when it has stopped working and become destructive of everything else they hold dear. That is what happened to

Standard of living is a function of the speed at which money bounces back and forth in your economy. Velocity, not volume, determines how well off you are.

alism, and ambitious war), the small town of Wörgl reduced its unemployment by 25 percent and the town government used the money it raised in tax stamps for public works. It built bridges and improved roads. When 300 other towns began to adopt the Wörgl system, the Austrian central bank stepped in and declared it illegal. The case went to the Austrian Supreme Court and Wörgl, Austria—and the world economy—lost.

the Wörgl system, and any alternative money systems created today can expect to encounter similar opposition from cultural, political, and financial interests that are heavily invested in the status quo ante. Because of this, I would expect that many of the most successful experiments of the next

An Ithaca HOURS note.

Local Currencies

BY STEPHEN BURKE

Among local currency systems in the U.S., Ithaca Hours is one of the oldest, at 15 years, and most successful, with about 1,000 users in a town of 30,000 people.

As revolutionary as they might seem, local currencies have a long history in the U.S. There was no national paper currency in the U.S until late in the 19th century, and many communities employed their own local currencies for daily economic transactions.

The last era of widespread local currency use was in the Great Depression, when U.S. dollars were exceedingly scarce. A less severe, but general and real, scarcity

of dollars led to the development of Ithaca Hours in the early 1990s.

Ithaca is a small town in central New York. Located far from the financial hub of New York City, it's closer to the Rust Belt and Snow Belt cities of the northeast which have been ravaged by spiraling energy costs and vanishing jobs. Underemployment is a perennial problem in Ithaca, where a large workforce in a competitive work environment translates into low wages.

Ithaca Hours was planned as way to promote gainful work for people, without depending on dollars. The idea was to create a completely new revenue stream to facilitate economic transactions. People could earn and spend Hours with their neighbors, trading goods and services, saving their dollars for other purposes.

Ithaca Hours is a member-based organization. Anyone is welcome to use Hours. But members sustain the system with an annual fee of $10 (or its equivalent, one Hour). And members are the means for issuing Hours into the community: the $10 fee brings each member a disbursement of two Ithaca Hours. This provides seed money for each member to spend with other members and, with about 600 members currently, constitutes an infusion of about $12,000 into the community each year.

century will emerge clandestinely and only be revealed when they have become so encased with popular support that eradicating them would be difficult.

Today Professor Kennedy lives in Lebensgarten, one of the oldest and most successful ökodorfs (ecovillages) in Germany.

> *It was a game of musical chairs, and at the end of each month the music sped up, people spent Free Schillings like crazy, and the Wörgl economy boomed.*

For the past 30 years her work in complementary currencies, micro-enterprise, and local lending have been expanded into a global movement, much of it still below the surface. In writing my book, The Post-petroleum Survival Guide and Cookbook: Recipes for Changing Times (New Society Pub-

Author Albert Bates

lishers, 2006), I included the Wörgl recipe for economic resuscitation between my mother's recipes for skillet cornbread and sweet potato soup.

Albert Bates is an instructor at the Ecovillage Training Center at The Farm community in Summertown, Tennessee, and author of 11 books, on energy, climate, history, and law, including Shutdown: Nuclear Power on Trial *(1979),* Climate in Crisis: The Greenhouse Effect and What We Can Do *(1990), and* Post-Petroleum Survival Guide and Cookbook: Recipes for Changing Times *(New Society Publishers, Fall, 2006).*

Members also benefit from inclusion in an annual Directory—an "alternative yellow pages"—which is often where members (and non-members, too) will look first for goods and services. The Directory is also online, so can accommodate new entries all year long, unlike the standard Yellow Pages.

At first, the Ithaca Hours' system primarily consisted of people trading services. Businesses largely were wary of accepting a currency that they couldn't use for nonlocal expenses, such as paying utilities, taxes, and goods purchased from outside the community. But as membership in Ithaca Hours grew, businesses realized the advantages of access to a large group of people with a currency they were eager to spend. Increasing numbers of local businesses began accepting Ithaca Hours, since accepting a local currency is a way to attract new, loyal customers. Accepting a local currency provides a small, local business with a distinct advantage over non-local chain stores. And because each business is free to create its own acceptance policy, the business doesn't end up with too many Ithaca Hours notes that it can't spend. Most businesses accept a limited amount, or limited percentage, of Hours per transaction. But businesses that do a good deal of business in the community, and that wish to maximize the competitive advantage of Hours acceptance, can (and do) accept 100 percent Hours from a customer for selling their product or service.

In recent years, the strength of the Hours system has enabled the Ithaca Hours organization to offer interest-free loans to member businesses. The system also makes regular contributions to community groups for a gamut of philanthropic purposes.

Ithaca Hours has been recognized by economists for the value of its "multiplier effect"—multiplying economic transactions in the community and creating new ones, with its local scope. For example, an Ithaca Hour spent at a local music store will soon be spent at another local business, while a dollar spent at a Borders chain will mostly likely soon leave the community for the bookstore chain's corporate headquarters elsewhere.

There is also an ineffable community-building aspect to using local currencies. Local people spending Hours find that the very act of spending them leads to conversations and camaraderie, something spending government-issued dollars don't do. They also show the power of a community to solve even seemingly intractable problems (shortage of money!) by taking creative action, together.

Stephen Burke is president of the Board of Directors of Ithaca Hours in Ithaca, New York.

BY GWYNELLE DISMUKES

THE FARM COMMUNITY

*Potluck meals in community are one of the most
obvious ways to "get back more than you put in,"
in terms of food, good company,
and a sense of connection.*

WHEN A DOLLAR IS WORTH MORE THAN 100 CENTS

The principles of Kwanzaa, the African-American holiday celebrated every winter (December 26th to January 1st), are based on concepts of communal living observed in traditional African villages. I find it only natural that the fourth principle of Kwanzaa, *Ujamaa*, which means "cooperative economics," should manifest readily in an intentional community setting. From potluck meals to shared property taxes, the byproducts of a communal lifestyle include benefits that may not be measurable in dollar amounts, but which nevertheless contribute to the group's overall well-being. It's a case of, "You put in a little; you get back a lot."

Take the potluck meal, one of the most obvious ways of getting back more than you put in. At The Farm community in central Tennessee where I live, we are blessed with women who have published cookbooks and pioneered vegetarian dishes for more than 30 years. You always get a gourmet meal when you invest the time (and an appetizer or dessert) in a community meeting, fundraising party, or holiday event here at The Farm. House-raising parties are a way in which we reduce construction costs, share labor and expertise (and once again, good food), and boost community spirits all at the same time—a regular 3 for 1!

In many communities, and certainly here at The Farm, businesses, nonprofits, schools, and other organizations directly support community members by providing employment and marketing opportunities. Frequently community needs are supported as well by member-owned businesses. For example, at The Farm we have a member-owned recycling service, a retail food store, and a staffed meeting facility, to name a few. Through avenues such as these, money is circulated through the community, benefiting its members within the wider economic framework.

At the same time, intangible aspects of support generated by communal living add another dimension to the concept of cooperative economics. In mainstream culture, dollars and cents are passed often unseen from one party to another, through online buying or by mail or by phone.

always more than one family or individual could afford to maintain for themselves. Those of us who have chosen the community lifestyle gain the use of land and facilities for which we pay only a fraction of the cost of ownership and provide a fraction of the labor required for upkeep. Pooling our resources in most cases allows us to have more assets, amenities, and time than we could possibly attain on our own, thus enriching each of us individually and raising the quality of life for the whole group.

I find it only natural that the fourth principle of Kwanzaa, Ujamaa, *"cooperative economics," manifests readily in an intentional community setting.*

But in an intentional community, even monetary exchanges have a face: human relationship is added to the transaction, and the passing of paper or coinage from hand to hand has a personal story attached, one which adds to the life of the people involved. In this context, money can be seen for what it really is—a representation of energy, a means of exchange, and a medium of conversation about resources and how they are used.

Whatever a community's shared physical property—be it a house or neighborhood in an urban area, or many acres and natural surroundings in a rural area—the property is almost

In my own case, a single mother with two children, I've been blessed to acquire equity in a large house, something I could not imagine doing in the outside world. Here at The Farm I was able to take over a house that was up for grabs when the last owner left, a house in such disrepair that no one wanted to take it on; in fact, many people tried to discourage me from getting into it at the beginning. But with credit cards, personal loans, and a young carpenter who was grateful for the work, I could afford to patch up the 25-year-old, 5-bedroom, 2-story house and make it livable for the next 5 years. In that time, my "mortgage" has consisted of paying back the initial rehab costs plus keeping up with current maintenance needs. The Farm has equity in the house, and of course the house can only be transferred to a Farm member; but it seems to me that these restrictions merely balance the great good fortune of my technically "owning" a house, a significant material resource which I can leverage in any number of creative ways.

Of course, creativity has been a hallmark of The Farm from the beginning, visible in the school buses converted into comfortable homes on wheels by resourceful hippies who joined the Caravan from San Francisco to Tennessee. In the 30-some

Cooperative economics is also demonstrated through work parties, like this wall-raising party.

years since then, cooks like Barb Bloomfield *(Soup's On!, More Fabulous Beans)* and Louise Hagler *(Miso Cookery, Tofu Quick and Easy)* have created recipes shared with thousands of people through their books, and they continue to serve up new improvisations of ingredients and presentation to fortunate family and friends here. Veggie Deli owner/operators Roberta Kachinsky and Ramona Christopherson have created their own version of ice bean, a frozen soy dessert that makes summer worth sweating through. The Ecovillage Training Center has recently created the "hipitat" (hippie habitat), a round cob building in varying sizes, generally constructed by students and interns during natural building courses. Frank

An on-site store selling food and sundries to community members, like The Farm Store, is another example of cooperative economics.

Michaels, owner of Mushroom People here at The Farm, not only offers mail order supplies for mushroom growers, but also turns out designs for solar showers, cookers, dehydrators, and greenhouses. Plenty International is a Farm-based NGO that provides a creative solution to poverty in developing countries by teaching people how to make and use soy products. There is certainly no lack of creativity on the Farm, and we apply these inventions and ideas to managing our individual resources in the communal setting.

enrich the individual by providing him or her with a personal reward; it benefits everybody by helping to maintain the swimming hole, for example, or paying for our weekly newsletter. I myself am terribly math-challenged, and I can't even begin to understand the figures, but our treasurer, Barbara Jefferson, puts out these beautiful reports that seem to indicate, bottom line, that we are at least pledging ourselves into keeping our heads—and maybe even our shoulders—above water. We definitely have a chance to swim. My

---

I've been blessed to acquire equity in a large house, something I could not imagine doing in the outside world.

For example, labor for The Farm can be traded for community dues, and residents/members can submit proposals for services they can provide in exchange for their dues. People have paid their dues by pruning shrubs, doing research, and archiving Farm materials. Members have the chance to create a job for themselves if they have an idea about something the community needs that they can offer.

Within the context of shared resources, any financial transaction can be more than the sum of its cash. The Farm operates on a pledge system: all members are expected to pay a minimum monthly amount which covers basic community expenses, and they can pledge more for additional services. Any extra money thus pledged does more than

interpretation is that the magic of community, like the miracle of the loaves and the fishes, somehow multiplies whatever it is that we put into the pot. Somehow, value is added to a dollar when it's shared in a conscious setting of community.

So for me, having my own house represents not at all a symbol of individual achievement or status. Rather, it is an opportunity for me to further share and contribute to the proverbial pot. When I presented my proposal to the board to acquire this house five years ago, I outlined a plan to create group housing on the site, and in the last few months I have begun to dimly see a way to actually begin moving in that direction. It won't be all cash—although certainly some things will require money or other firm payment—but will also probably include volunteer effort, trades, grants, even student participation. As I remain open to ideas, holding the space for some kind of neo-communal living, I know that the universe will respond and eventually things will fall into place. And what would ordinarily be a simple quest for individual shelter on my part is turning into a project to create a sustainable cluster, using the materials and resources at hand, and involving other like-minded individuals with the ability to expand on the vision and help bring it into manifestation.

In mainstream culture, the major part of most people's wages or salaries goes into their house: for a mortgage, furniture, appliances, and entertainment systems— all the things that "house"

With volunteer labor, community projects cost less. Here, two community members refinish a picnic table for a new children's area at The Farm.

THE FARM COMMUNITY

implies in our consumer society. But ultimately, it is a material investment and nothing more; when it is time to move on, the house is converted into a transaction until the next owner puts a saddle on their back and is ridden by the house to work and pay for its continued existence. By con-

For that matter, some people find that a communal lifestyle actually reduces stress and increases health, so it could be argued that we are saving money on medical care. A great many people both in urban and rural communities enjoy a huge reduction in transportation costs as they are able to work, buy groceries, and visit friends all within walking distance. The benefits of community compound quickly when we begin thinking of all the ways in which we are saving money as a result of living and working together.

As an exercise for practicing *Ujamaa*, I like to explain the idea of the *susu*. Based on a Nigerian custom, the *susu* is a group of people that rotates payments to one another each month, so that everyone gets a windfall whenever their turn rolls around. As I presented the idea in my book *Practicing Kwanzaa Year Round*, the *susu* is intended as a way for people—and especially African Americans— to connect with traditions from the African continent in a way that is meaningful in today's westernized world.

Within the context of shared resources, any financial transaction can be more than the sum of its cash.

---

trast, the older houses here in our community have a history that will last as part of the history of this collective, and renovating or maintaining a house adds a little more time for that history to unfold within walls that have held a lot of good energy over the last 20-30 years. Building a new house adds to the community's overall assets, so new houses, too, have value beyond their market price or their usefulness to their individual owners. Most important, because people here enjoy a more flexible work environment, nobody has to feel like they are "working for their house," unless, of course, they choose to do so. Since our lifestyle at The Farm is based more on spiritual values than material features, our members can take on less of the drive and obsession that can come with home ownership in the outside world.

In a sense, an intentional community *is* a *susu*, generating financial as well as emotional and spiritual windfalls for its members. An intentional community demonstrates cooperative economics in the broadest sense, and it is a model that our beleaguered world governments would do well to appreciate and consider as the next step in an economically sustainable future.❀

Gwynelle Dismukes is a writer and editor who has lived at The Farm since 1998. She is author of Black 2 the Future, Practicing Kwanzaa Year Round, *and* Afrikan Alkhemy: Spiritual and Soul Transformation in America. *Her books are available from the Farm-based business Mail Order Catalog: www.healthy-eating.com/gwynellebooks.htm.*

ABOVE: *Glen Ivy community has a thriving hot springs and spa business.*
BELOW: *The now-defunct Lila Commune, New Mexico, 1970.*

SOCIAL CLASS & MONEY IN COMMUNITY

BY ALLEN HANCOCK

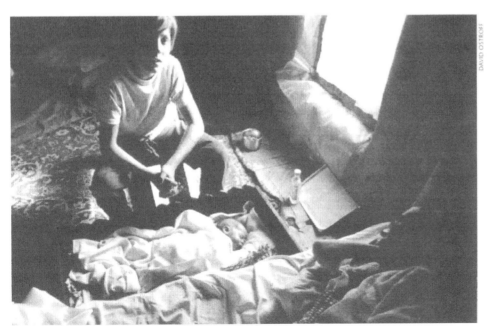

"WHERE DID YOU GET the money to start your community?" For several years, I replied nervously to this frequently asked question by saying, "We have an anonymous lender," knowing that I stood out like a windmill on the prairie. I kept hoping that no one would find out that I was the anonymous lender, fearful that if others found out that I had inherited money they would treat me differently, try to fundraise from me, or show disrespect for the mixed blessing that comes with having more money than others. I was so cautious that many of the members in our close-knit intentional community didn't even know my secret.

Over time, I realized that my fears were unfounded. I began telling folks that *I* was the anonymous lender. To my surprise, very little changed in my relationships with others. Instead of seeing me as the "owner" of the community as I had feared, people often commended me for having vision and integrity to use my money in such a way. As I became more comfortable revealing my secret, I ran into more and more people who had also used their private money (often from inheritances) to help create intentional communities. Interestingly, I found that they too felt trepidation in talking about it.

I began to see a pattern of ideas that people hold onto to protect themselves from their fears about money. Underneath much of it lie class issues. Unlike gender or race, socioeconomic class remains virtually hidden in the United States, compared to other social distinctions. A person's class status is less visibly apparent than gender or race and distinctions in class are not simply financial, since education, values, attitudes, and social standing are also parts of the puzzle. This issue is further complicated because a person can have parents from different class backgrounds and can change class

15

identity at different times in life. In addition, financial factors may mix with cultural patterns in ways that seem contradictory. For example, upper middle-class New Englanders repair items that many working class people would throw out.

What I find most insidious about class distinctions are the limiting messages and ideas that each of us carries with us that limit our fullest potential, and which keep us from being closer to one another in community.

People from working-class and poor backgrounds for example, often feel incapable or stupid. In meetings, they often remain quiet—fearful that they won't be able to say anything "right." They will often avoid intellectual discussions or planning in favor of "getting on with things." For better or worse, this group may find the voluntary simplicity practiced in many communities unappealing. The next time someone brings home a used couch for a common space,

consider the implications for someone who may have lived with hand-me-downs all his or her life. We have much to learn from working class and raised-poor people; for example, they frequently have close ties with families and friends (often out of economic necessity) that can serve as models to intentional community.

Middle-class patterns are a little harder to detect. Society encourages people with this background to have aspirations of affluence and not to rock the boat (if you do, you might lose your job). This often translates into peacekeeping behavior. Notice the people in your group who avoid taking a position on controversial issues or who have alliances with many types of people. What do they get from taking on this role? What can we learn from people who know how to mediate differences? Also notice whether middle-class community members intellectualize interpersonal differences by discussing

theories, paradigms, or models instead of showing emotion. This can drive a wedge between them and working-class members.

People who come from upper-class families (sometimes called the "owning class") tend to find many ways of isolating and distancing themselves from others. This can mean holding on to secrets about money (as I did); confidently asserting that they're OK when in reality they're feeling angry, hurt, confused, scared, and so on; or using their affluence to create physical separation from others. Some co-housing communities comprised of more affluent households may find their members using their separate dwellings as a way of shielding themselves from the challenges of living together.

Once you notice how you and others act out issues around class, how can you minimize classism in everyday life? Here are some suggestions.

• Put yourself in situations both

Overview: Social Classes in America Today

You may not agree with these categories or descriptions; they are simply offered to stimulate your thinking.

Very Poor people lack basic needs generation after generation; most are uneducated or unemployed.

Poor people lack sufficient money to meet basic needs such as food and health care. Many have dropped out of school and are unable to secure ongoing work. Many do not have bank accounts and cannot qualify for credit.

Working Class people usually get their basic needs met, but they often have to save up for and choose between simple luxuries, such as eating out versus buying new clothes for the kids. In the past few went to college; now many go to vocational school or community college and hold "blue" or "pink" collar jobs (e.g., cashier, clerical worker).

Many **Middle Class** people go to college (often state schools) and hold "white collar" jobs or become owners of small businesses. Many buy modest homes, although this now often requires a two-income family. They save up for luxuries (e.g., summer camp, a new car).

Many **Upper Middle Class** people go to private schools, pay people to work in their homes (e.g., housekeepers, gardeners), and take a fair amount of luxury for granted. They hold "professional jobs" such as architect or doctor. Children often receive inheritances from parents.

Owning Class people grow up in families that have substantial ownership of private businesses, land, or shares of stock in corporations. Their adult lives frequently involve substantial time and responsibility in managing their own financial assets. Most have sufficient income to support their families without working.

Ruling Class people not only have great wealth, but also considerable power. Many have been groomed from childhood to take positions of great influence in business, politics, and/or the community. They often have great political influence behind the scenes.—A.H.

within and outside your group where you'll meet people from different class backgrounds. For example, take public transit or attend an opera in a major city. Notice what feelings and thoughts (particularly judgments) you have in these situations. Learn as much as you can by observing and interacting to find things you share in common with people of various backgrounds.

• Discuss your class background with friends. Ask about their class backgrounds if they feel comfortable talking about them. If they don't feel comfortable, what can you learn from their reluctance?

• Pay attention to the kinds of tasks and work you and others do. Is the kind of work you're most comfortable with associated with a particular class? Challenge yourself and others to take on a variety of jobs, including physical labor, administration, and decision making. Take time to ask for support from others if doing (or just thinking about doing) unfamiliar tasks brings up discomfort.

• Listen to the language people use as well as how vocal or quiet people are in different meetings, while socializing, or in confrontations. Do some people speak with a sense of authority or use technical jargon? Are others timid in speaking up when they have something important to say? Do some say whatever comes to their minds? Assess how a person's class background may affect language patterns and how, in turn, that affects group dynamics. What can you learn from each others' use of language?

• Notice what patterns people have in relationship to earning, spending, and saving money. To what extent do their behaviors and attitudes reflect the expectations of people from their class backgrounds?

• Consider how former members of your group may have felt separate from those "within your circle" because of their class identity. How can you avoid the subtle ways of discriminating against people from different class backgrounds?

• Evaluate what privileges you may have; for example, connections to professionals, college education, a vacation home. Can you use those privileges to help empower less privileged people? Do you enjoy any privileges at the expense of others? If so, what can you do to use these privileges to minimize classism?

• Recognize that classism (as well as racism, sexism, homophobia, and so forth) is so entrenched in our society that despite our best efforts, we will unknowingly help perpetuate class segregation. Be easy on yourself and others.

• Consider Re-evaluation Co-counseling (RC) or other methods of personal growth as way of working through the emotional challenges of class issues. There are RC classes and support groups, for example, for working class, middle class, and owning class folks. For more information, write Rational Island Publishers, Box 2081, Main Office, Seattle, WA 98111.

If we are successful in overcoming our personal and interpersonal patterns around class, we will be more trusting and compassionate with each other. We will see that we have similar dreams and be more willing try bold, creative ways of using our individual and collective finances for the benefit of all. Who knows, perhaps the person sitting next to you on the bus inherited a million dollars and wants to create intentional community. Ω

Allen Hancock is co-founder of Du-má community in Eugene, Oregon, and publisher of More Than Money, *a quarterly journal for people with earned and inherited wealth who want to use their money in ways that are socially responsible. For information about* More Than Money, *contact him at 2244 Alder Street, Eugene, OR 97405, or call 800-255-4903.*

The Walnut St. Co-op is located near the university in Eugene, Oregon.

Our Community Revolving Loan Fund:

How Walnut Street Co-op Financed Its Property

BY TREE BRESSEN

Community revolving loan funds are an amazing tool. When we converted our house to cooperative ownership, no bank was willing to offer us a mortgage. Out of necessity, we searched for alternatives, and succeeded in purchasing our 9-bedroom home in Eugene, Oregon thanks to approximately 20 friends who gave us private loans. This is a fantastic model for alternative financing, a do-it-yourself empowerment that shifts power away from conventional institutions toward creating a better world. This description is written to enable other groups to benefit from the knowledge our co-op gained from creating this fund.

We have a contract with each lender that specifies how much money is being loaned, for how long, at what interest rate, and any other terms. Our usual parameters are a $5,000 minimum loan, 5-year minimum time, and no more than six percent interest. We aim to be flexible, however, and every contract is a bit different. For example, one loan requires us to maintain an advisory team. Our lenders have been very generous with us:

some lent at zero percent interest, others at two to three percent, and a few are using simple interest rather than compound interest; also some were able to commit for 10 to 15 years. We offer a way for people to invest in alignment with their values and our lenders appreciate that.

Our loans are in the range of $5,000 to 20,000, except for one $120,000 loan from a person who met us when we had already raised over half the money we needed and offered to cover the rest.

Most of our loans are amortized at 30 years, which makes the payments affordable. If you are unfamiliar with this term, amortization means that the payments are stretched out over a really long time. That's how people of limited means are able to buy something big like a house. Thirty years is a typical amortization for a standard home mortgage from a bank. However, unlike a bank, most individuals cannot predict the course of their lives 30 years ahead and therefore are not prepared to commit their assets for that long. So instead the way our loans work is that we

18

make small payments during the five years, acting as if it were a 30-year loan. But then at the end of the five years, we have to pay the entire remaining balance due—this is called a balloon payment.

That means that every five years our community will go through a refinancing cycle. We'll be asking each lender whether they'd like to turn the balance due on their loan back into the fund to lend to us again, or whether they want the money back. We'll need to replace all the loans that people want repaid, either with money from new lenders or with increased loans from existing lenders. This is somewhat risky, because if we were unable to find adequate new financing we'd have to sell our property to repay the loans. However, that risk seems very worth it to us, and after our experience so far we are reasonably confident in our ability to do the refinancing—after all, we were able to do it the first time around, and over time we are only going to become a more attractive investment because the community will have more equity in the property and a proven track record of repayment.

Our payments are quarterly rather than monthly, to reduce paperwork. With the exception of our one large loan, the loans to our co-op are unsecured. That means they are not officially attached to our property in county records, in the event that the co-op dissolves and the house is sold. This is partly because we wanted all of our lenders beyond the one large loan to share an "equal second" position: meaning that if the house was sold and the money wasn't enough to pay back all the loans, everyone would get a proportion equal to the portion of their investment, to be fair. But when loans are secured with the property, they get priority in the sequence in which they were recorded with the county, so that all of A's loan is paid off before B gets anything.

Members of the Walnut Street Co-op include founder/owners and tenent/residents

> *We attend to our relationships with our lenders; they are our friends and not just a source of financing.*

In order to give everyone an equal position we would have had to form a whole separate legal entity, and even then the lawyer we talked to wasn't sure it was doable. Also, having 20 separate loans attached to a property is very complicated, especially when the lenders change over the years. So instead, our loans are unsecured, and the contract with each lender explains that they are in an equal second position with other lenders.

Some of the loans have co-op members signed as personal guarantors. That means that if the co-op fails to make payments, each of those guarantors can be held responsible for the entire remaining balance of the loan. But even with that, what it really comes down to is that this whole community revolving loan fund deal is based on trust. Our lenders understand that we are committed having integrity in our relationship with them, and that while we don't expect our co-op to fall apart, if it does we will do our utmost to fulfill our financial obligations. If the co-op dissolves, outside investors get paid in full before any co-op residents get paid anything. Because our house appraised at nearly $50,000 more than we paid for it and real estate values in our town are rising, it is extremely unlikely that we'd be unable to repay all the loans even if we did have to sell the property.

Our lenders come from a variety of sources. Some are active folks in the communities movement who believe in creating more intentional communities. Some are personal friends who felt moved to support a particular individual here. Some are supporters of a wonderful nonprofit based here in our house, Tom Atlee's Co-Intelligence Institute. We also received support from several organizations in the communities movement.

We attend to our relationships with our lenders; they are our friends and not just a source of financing. We strive to be honest with them, offering genuine appreciation and

Author, Tree Bressen

practical information without distortion or descent into puffery. We try to visit them when we are in their locale, send them a quarterly newsletter, explain to newer housemates who they are as people, and so on. Our lenders are a valuable part of our wider community and we are very grateful for their continued support.

When we started this fund, we created a beautiful, well-written packet that explained our project to prospective lenders. Our packet included the following components:

1. Our vision of what our community is doing and why it matters;
2. History of our project and community;
3. Business plan;
4. Biographies of the core group;
5. International co-op principles (also known as the Rochdale principles), explanation of what a co-op is and of our type of community (limited-equity co-op);
6. Testimonial letter from a respected leader in the intentional communities movement;
7. Photos of the house (interior and exterior, with core group members in some of the pictures);
8. Form for enrolling support (loans, donations, and more);
9. Self-addressed stamped envelope.

> *You are offering lenders a service and an opportunity. You are helping them to live out their values in the world.*

If you are setting out to create a Community Revolving Loan Fund for your intentional community or other project, here is what i advise:

1. Believe in what you are doing and share your passion.
2. Have everyone in your project make a list of everyone they know that has $5,000 or more (or whatever your minimum investment is) that they might be able to lend. Hopefully you will be surprised by how many names are on the list. You won't end up asking everyone on that list, but it gets you started seeing the possibilities.
3. Remember that you are offering lenders a service and an opportunity. You are helping them to live out their values in the world. At 3 percent interest you would be providing a higher profit than a savings account and a more reliable profit than many other investments.
4. Keep the trust. Some people loaned to us based on one conversation without ever seeing the packet, simply because they believed in the person asking. At first i was shocked by this, but i came to understand that trust is the central element in a lender's decision. Be honest, transparent, and above all, always act with integrity.

Walnut St.'s Community Revolving Loan Fund was inspired and assisted by a similar entity at Los Angeles Eco-Village.

Note: Tree Bressen treats the first-person pronoun "I" as no more or less important than any other word by keeping it lower-case when it appears midsentence.

In addition to being a founding member of Walnut St. Co-op, Tree consults on group process with intentional communities and other nonprofits on how to have lively, productive, and connecting meetings. Her website, www.treegroup.info, offers free tools and resources. Walnut St. Co-op's website is: www.icetree.com/walnut.

Other Possible Financing Sources

1. **Institute for Community Economics (ICE):** Their bureaucratic wheels turn slowly and they require huge amounts of documentation, but they can lend over $100,000 if your project is structured as a land trust or limited equity cooperative.
2. **PEACH (Protected Equity Accessible for Community Health):** The member communities of the Federation of Egalitarian Communities (FEC) operate their own health risk fund, a portion of which is available for investment in intentional communities. This is a great cooperative resource. Contact the PEACH administrator, Laird Schaub, for more information at laird@ic.org or 660-883-5545.
3. **Sunrise Credit Union** is the only credit union in the U.S. based in an intentional community (Sunrise Ranch in Loveland, Colorado). Credit unions, especially young ones, are closely monitored by federal agencies so they are somewhat limited in their flexibility, however they offered us a substantial loan if we proffered a qualified cosigner.
4. **Permaculture Credit Union:** This is an even newer credit union, and they are not set up to lend in very many states yet, but you can contact them to find out if they are a resource in your area.
5. **NASCO (North American Students of Cooperation)** lends money to cooperatives that fit current lending parameters, through their CCDC development company.
6. You can try asking other intentional communities and intentional community organizations, particularly ones in your region.
7. In theory the National Cooperative Bank (NCB) should be a source of financing for projects like this, but we were told we were too small for them to even consider. However, if you are converting an apartment building in New York to a co-op, they'd probably be interested.   —T.B.

Inventing a Rural Economy,
Business by Business

How The Farm Lost its Communal Subsidy and Formed a Stable Economy in Its Place

BY DOUGLAS STEVENSON

In 1983, when The Farm community in Tennessee changed form a communal economy to a private economy of independent incomes, we members suddenly needed to generate personal income to support ourselves. We were also expected to meet our obligation to contribute toward the maintenance and development expenses of a large community infrastructure. During this difficult transition we had many

It can often take years to build a member-owned business so that it's truly profitable.

over again. The rules were different and it was time to take what we had learned and see how we could apply it to changing times. Many previously subsidized services fell by the wayside as people struggled to get on their feet. Hundreds of people left the community to seek jobs in cities around the country. After a few years our population, once 1200, stabilized at around 250. Those of us who remained had found a way to generate an income in rural, middle Tennessee, and we were committed to continued living in the community.

Located 70 miles from Nashville, few of our members have been willing to commute the hour and a half drive each way in order to take jobs there. Job opportunities in the small towns nearest The Farm have been limited as well. In the 20 years since our conversion to an individually based income, the sources for our economy have fallen into a few distinct categories: unskilled jobs, skilled jobs, and member-owned service-based, manufacturing, and mail-order businesses.

Getting Started

It can often take many years to build a member-owned business in community to the point that it is truly profitable or able to sustain a paid staff and several employees. Quite often community members must rely on outside jobs to guarantee themselves a steady income. However, by developing professional skills, individual community members can in many instances earn a better-than-average salary while avoiding the stress of starting a busi-

ness. We have many members with medical degrees or professional licenses of some type, including quite a few registered nurses, a nurse practitioner, a physician's assistant, an emergency medical administrator, and a lactation consultant—services for which there is always a strong demand. Other types of outside jobs vary widely, from people who provide office and accounting services to massage therapy and legal services.

Fortunately telecommuting is now a reality. If community members can provide a service that can be delivered via the Internet or in some sort of digital form, their physical location can become irrelevant. Authors, editors, accountants, designers, and database managers can all make a living from a rural location. For over 15 years I have written articles for a magazine in California from my cabin in Tennessee. It has been nearly 10 years since my editor and I have seen each other face to face.

Quite naturally many community members rely on the building trades to earn a living. This is also one of the easiest businesses to start that can support more than one person. A van or truck, an assortment of power tools, and a few business cards can be all that's necessary to jump right into a fairly respectable income. Indeed some of our most successful community members at The Farm are people who developed their skills and reputation, and eventually became building contractors. These folks now provide work for several crews, usually managing several large building projects simultaneously. Their business has been one of our community's primary employers.

Many small business entrepreneurs will create companies that focus on a particular skill or service. From heating and cooling to computer repair, the skilled professional that can fix, install, or satisfy a need can develop a business serving the broader local community. These types of businesses usually start as sole proprietorships before expanding to need additional help and employees.

Start-Up Businesses

The costs and time it takes to build a business can vary greatly. Unless you have access to a substantial amount of money and venture capital, a community business must often begin as a "bootstrap"

A Farm workshop held at a community yoga studio.

questions: Which services could the community afford now that it would have to pay people for their labor? How much was the community willing to subsidize the overhead of running those operations? Could people with valuable but highly specialized skills find employment within the community's few businesses or in the local area? How far would people be willing to drive in order to get jobs so they could still live in the community? What types of businesses and means of support could we develop from our rural location?

Although The Farm had undergone 10 years of pioneering development, in many ways "the Changeover" was like starting operation investing a lot of sweat equity.

One good example is the business based on a craft product. Using inexpensive tools and raw materials, craft producers create their products at home, and then hit the road, displaying them at appropriate crafts fairs. Often the craftsperson spends the winter months in their shop and does most of the marketing during the warm weekends of summer. Those seeking a year-round market may move on to warmer states like Florida or the southwest during winter months. During the late 1980s The Farm's reputation was spread far and wide by a member who sold tie-dyed tee-shirts all over the South and Midwest while his family stayed at home and produced the shirts. Of course the disadvantage of the crafts business can be that this work takes the person away from home during the growing season and when the community is likely to have more of its own events and activities. The life on the road is not for everyone. Some communities, such as East Wind and Twin Oaks (so I understand), handle this by utilizing rotating crews that take turns on the road or displaying products at fairs.

While craftspeople produce products to sell, true manufacturing takes this method of generating income to a new level. The product is likely to be more complex to produce, with numerous steps or work stations, and specialized equipment may be required. Unless the company controls both production and retail sales, chances are the manufacturer will need to develop a customer base of stores that sell their product or utilize a distributor that sells a line of similar products to the appropriate retail outlets or directly to the end customers. If demand for the product is strong, the manufacturing business can rely on a few sales people that go outside the community to acquire contracts and distribution deals while most of the workers stay back at the homestead.

SE International is an electronics manufacturing firm owned by a Farm member that makes Geiger counters. The units were initially developed as part of the community's protest against nuclear power plants. Now some 20 years later, the Geiger counters are valuable tools utilized by hospitals, emergency rescue, "hazmat" (hazardous material emergency crews), and a variety of other industries.

The company employs over 15 other community members in a wide range of skills, from office management and shipping to product assembly and calibration.

Mail-Order Businesses

It would seem that the mail order business is made to order for communities. Customers receive direct mail catalogs or visit a website, therefore the company's actual location isn't important. Community members working at a mail order business take phone orders or retrieve sales from "shopping carts" built into the company's website. UPS and Federal Express can deliver the company's products to the customer in a few days or even the next morning. All it takes is inventory, a healthy demand, and savvy marketing skills. However the mail-order business can take

How far would people be willing to drive in order to get jobs so they could still live in the community?

many years to develop as the company builds a reputation and a sufficient customer base. Of course there is always the risk of new and better-financed competition or that the line of products goes out of vogue. The better mail-order businesses develop loyal, repeat customers who

come back to buy again and again.

The Mail Order Catalog at The Farm was started initially as a retail outlet for books produced by the community's publishing company as well as a few packaged food products. As a sideline the community members who owned and managed the company began purchasing the "seconds" of books from other publishers. Sales of these discounted books surpassed those of new, full-priced books. Later they added food products and these eventually took over as the primary revenue stream. Everyone eats but not everyone has time to go shopping or has access to specialized foods. Production, distribution, or direct sales of food and food products will always be valuable, and can be a substantial income source for a community business.

As appealing as the mail-order business might be, it is not without difficulties. Catalogs can be expensive to print. Mailing costs continue to rise. Increasingly greater amounts of catalogs must be sent out to produce a much smaller percentage of sales.

Display or classified ads in specialized magazines, though expensive, may be necessary to reach a target market and let them know about the mail-order products and catalog. Initially the business owner might be required to purchase mailing lists in order to jump-start sales. Web-based catalogs have their own set of problems, primarily how to get noticed in an ever-widening sea of digital domains. Generally speaking, the print and print catalogs work best when used as two parts of a whole. The Farm's mailorder catalog company promotes their web site in their print catalog, and many people utilize their website as a convenient way to place their order.

Workshops and Education

Many communities rely on or plan to develop educational workshops and relaxing retreat facilities, thus bringing cash flow and customers directly to the community. However, it's important to match the people the community is trying to attract with the comfort level of its facilities. Is it providing individual rooms with all the amenities or will the participants be expected to camp or live in rustic conditions? There has to be a balance between the community's ability to deliver information or experiences demanded by the market, and the accommodations people are willing to accept. Generally speaking, the more rustic or dorm-like the community's accommodations, the

less participants will be willing to pay. Careful planning is required to develop an operations budget and a marketing plan that brings in a sufficient number of properly targeted workshop participants.

Again the marketing plan is usually based on direct mail and display advertising, catalogs, and brochures. These days, traditional forms of advertising are enhanced by the business's ability to direct interested parties to a website where they can get more information, register, and even pay by credit card.

Although we host a variety of workshops at The Farm, our midwifery assistant training programs have proven to be the most successful, probably because they are a kind of training that can be found

The Making of a Community Entrepreneur

When I came to The Farm as a youth of 19 with no real skills, I felt drawn to join the radio crew. The Farm used ham radio to communicate with its members on affiliated small farms all over the country and its relief volunteers around the world. As I studied for my ham radio license, I also learned electronics and electronics repair, and became the communications person in Guatemala for Plenty International, our community's relief and development organization.

When I returned to the States in 1980, The Farm was beginning to realize it needed to establish businesses that could really support us. Our ham radio/electronics crew designed and began producing our first Geiger counter, the "Nukebuster," confident that there would be a demand for this important safety product. I oversaw the assembly and quality control. But during that first year, although we were working really hard, we weren't generating much in the way of real dollars for the community. I grew frustrated.

The author at work at Village Media.

I wanted to change jobs, so I was assigned to work with a friend on the crew who was researching a book about a new kind of electronics hardware, the satellite dish. I recognized the potential of this new entertainment phenomenon to be developed into a business serving the local area. I loaded the dish and a home-made receiver on to a trailer and went off to the county fair in search of prospective buyers.

Two fairs later, I had sold a dish to a local radio station so they could receive news and sports from a satellite feed, a home system to a local businessman, and a four- receiver installation

for our town's Holiday Inn. This was two years before our community's Changeover in 1983, when all Farm members would be required to earn their own income and support. Suddenly we (myself and my new business partner) had a real business, selling satellite systems right and left while providing training and employment for as many Farm members as possible.

At the time of the Changeover, because we'd started this community business we became its owners; we were two of the lucky members that had already figured out how to bring in an income. However, this was also a period of working 12 hour days, generally six days a week, and driving over 50,000 miles a year to sell and install our product. And although our company had over a half a million in cash flow and paid out $200,000 in salaries the second year after the Changeover, we had gotten ourselves over $50,000 in debt. We were paying off small bank loans and four vehicle notes, and driving our fleet of vehicles 200 miles a day when gas prices were going through the roof. Our whole operation started to crumble.

As the cable TV industry started scrambling their broadcast signals, sales of home satellite systems dropped significantly. My business partner left the community, and for the next several years I worked alone, providing service and maintenance for the systems that I had installed during our company's heyday. I had to consider my options. Most of my clients lived near Nashville, 70 miles away. Another satellite dealer in that location invited me to become his business partner, but it would mean moving.

nowhere else. The marketing efforts for these workshops benefit from Farm midwives having established a worldwide reputation. Attendees accept the simple accommodations without complaint and actually enjoy the bonding that takes place when sharing dormitory space. Promoted through a variety of display ads, the Farm midwives' week-long conferences are generally filled to capacity.

In our experience at The Farm, it has taken a variety of forms and approaches to create on-site member-owned businesses, both to suit the members involved and to create enough employment options for other members. This has also protected us as a community. Outside jobs come and go, and companies can rise and fall. People can get sick or experience trauma. But because our members' income sources are not based on only one type of service or product, our community economy is able to remain relatively secure and stable in spite of the roller coaster of our national economy. From the beginning, The Farm has called itself a school of change. The change from a communal economy to individual incomes has been its greatest challenge, one that continues to impact our growth and future development. Ω

Douglas Stevenson joined The Farm in 1973. He and his family spent two years in Guatemala in the late 1970s and recently worked six months in Belize volunteering with The Farm's organization Plenty International. He has served six years on The Farm's board of directors and four years as part of the membership committee. He is currently one of the community managers, organizing projects, community work-days, entertainment activities, and outreach. He owns Village Media,the company that assisted the FIC's Geoph Kozeny with his video documentary, Visions of Utopia"

Did I want leave The Farm and pursue this as a career, or continue the rural community lifestyle I loved?

About that time I ran into an old friend who had established a new career writing for some of the TV guide magazines that served the home satellite market. He introduced me to his editor at a trade show, and I agreed to write for the publishing company's trade journal for the home satellite dish industry. I wrote from my hands-on experience, providing how-to information on installing antenna towers and mini cable systems. Buoyed by this new form of supplemental income, I approached other trade magazines serving home satellite dish owners. I started spending less time on the road and more days at home, banging out words on one of the earliest home computers.

However these magazines were also feeling the downturn of the home satellite industry, and in an effort to follow the changing whims of the consumer marketplace, one publisher changed its focus to a new electronics device attracting a lot of attention, the video camcorder. "No problem," I said. "I can write about those." So I went out and purchased a camcorder and started writing about videoing my kids, videoing family vacations, how to edit home videos, and how people were using camcorders to make money.

I was intrigued. Maybe I could make money with video. I started reinvesting the profits from my satellite work into professional video equipment. I got lucky when I landed a job documenting a Farm member's reconstruction of a log cabin for the Army Corps of Engineers. His contract specified that the entire project had to be documented in video and with still pictures. I used the money I made from this job for my first video editing gear.

I got my biggest break when I became the advertising production company for the cable company serving three nearby towns. I started shooting and editing three to five commercials a week for local car dealers, furniture stores, and all kinds of local small

maybe I could make money with video

businesses. I started to have enough work to take on a new business partner. In addition to commercials, he and I also produced industrial marketing and training videos, and other small projects. Things were going along well, when all of a sudden the cable service, which was owned by a corporation in another state, decided to do all of their video production in their own in-house facility. Overnight we lost $50,000 a year in business.

It was hard, but we survived. I was still writing three or more articles a month, so we had some steady money coming in. Then I discovered a new technology on the horizon, the Internet. I took on my first job designing a web page before I even had the software in hand to get it done. For the next several months I buried myself in graphics and electronic shopping carts, learning by creating my own online catalog and building websites for a few local businesses and Farm-based nonprofits.

It's now been nearly 20 years now since the Changeover. Being in business for myself has had its ups and downs, both in terms of stress and income. However, it has also given me the freedom to choose my own hours and take time off when I needed to—in short, to control my own destiny. I've been the dad who could go on the school trips. I took the family back to Guatemala. I didn't have to ask for days off during the holidays. I could become more involved in our community, serving on The Farm's board of directors and organizing several small festivals. I've never had to punch a clock or wear a tie.

These days I write magazine articles, create and maintain web sites, and work on multimedia and video projects that interest me. My pace is a lot slower. I hardly ever leave The Farm. Many people have chosen a profession and then let that work lead them through life. I got to choose the intentional community I wanted and discovered the work that allowed me to live here.

—D.S.

Self-Reliance, Right Livelihood, and Economic "Realities": Finding Peace in Compromise

By Abeja Hummel

The dirt road to the valley floor winds its way through oak woodlands and past an enormous corporate vineyard. It bisects our neighbors' small horse farm and a massive overgrazed cattle ranch. If you had told me seven years ago that I'd have a 30-minute commute alone in my car to get to work twice a week, I'd have pointed out that I'd never even owned a car, that I don't need much money, and certainly don't work for "the man."

It's true, I have biked the road many times, and even driven our mule cart to town. Still, I've grown to really appreciate my biodiesel Jetta, and find I actually enjoy the time and space I get driving slowly through the countryside on my way to my bodywork practice in Boonville. Some would say I've grown up, some would say I've sold out. I would say that I have learned to compromise for love and a larger purpose. Having a child and living at Emerald Earth—a small, rural ecovillage in northern California—have taught me a lot about compromise.

We are incredibly blessed in that our land is owned—outright—by a nonprofit, so we aren't pouring money into a mortgage. As this is not currently an income-sharing community, we strive to keep the costs low for residents, and share the values of right livelihood and self-reliance. We are deeply engaged in rediscovering an interconnected, regenerative relationship with our land. We produce or wildcraft much of our own food, and sell or trade the surplus to neighbors for things we don't have. Our kitchen is usually packed with fresh, local, healthy, nutrient-dense foods. Processed, packaged, and sugary foods arrive only with unindoctrinated guests.

The cows and goats produce way more milk than we can consume, which we share with friends and turn into cheese and yogurt—all grass fed and higher quality than almost anything you can buy in a store. The chickens move around, cleaning and fertilizing our gardens and pastures and giving us in return delicious eggs with deep orange yolks. Our gardens pump out amazing organic produce. And on top of that, people from all over (though mostly the San Francisco Bay area) pay us to come to our community to take our workshops in natural building and other land-based practices.

So why is it, then, that I'm getting into my car twice a week and driving to town? Why is it that most residents here find it essential to have a well-paying off-site job, some savings, and little to no debt?

In the mythology of America, families can be completely supported by a successful small farm. Yet we find ourselves walking a line between radical self-sufficiency and the realities of the dominant culture's economic and social systems. We work jobs in town out of fear—must keep health insurance, must have car insurance, must pay debt. We also make money to pay for the fun things we still want from "out there"—a ski trip this winter, a new guitar, a music festival. So we work for someone or something else—taking our time and energy away from the vision we hold for ourselves and this land.

Our plan is to move towards the possibility that all residents can make a living on the land. We believe that a bounty of valuable goods and services can be gleaned in the process of revitalizing degraded topsoil, caring for the forests and creeks, collecting nature's abundance, and bringing life back towards the balance the native Pomo so carefully tended. This bounty includes milk and meat from goats that clear the underbrush from the thrice-logged tinderbox we see as an old-growth forest in the making. Proper management of our cows is rebuilding topsoil in our oak woodlands, as we watch the fertility and biodiversity increase over the years. We can envision a surplus of lumber—or at the very least firewood—resulting from a forestry plan that increases the health of the forest while decreasing the fire load. Mushrooms, acorns, and all sorts of other wild edibles offer themselves to us every year and we believe—as the Pomo have taught us—that wild things WANT to be respectfully gathered and used, and that their life cycles are benefited by that relationship.

I have a lot of time to think about these things, as I drive up and down the hill to work. I have considered abandoning my business in town many times and have experimented with various income sources from the land. Our first year here, my husband and I diligently went to the farmers' market with surplus fruit from ours and our neighbors' land, as well as wildcrafted mushrooms and seaweed. I also did chair massage. It was very socially rewarding and completely in line with our values. We made somewhere around $4 an hour for the harvesting and time at the market—we did not calculate in time spent caring for the fruit trees. The only real income derived from that time is the regular clients I gathered for my bodywork practice.

In America we are accustomed to buying food—as well as every other mass-produced commodity—cheaply. Selling the tastiest eggs you've ever tried at $6 a dozen, I would walk the line between red and black after figuring in the cost of supplemental organic feed. And that would come with a huge amount of work and folks complaining about my eggs being too expensive. Same math for the incredibly delicious fresh bread we bake in our wood-fired cob oven with local, organic, stone-ground wheat. (The saint who is growing the local wheat, I might add, is doing it as a labor of love at $1 a pound.) With time, good marketing, and cultivated relations with neighbors, however, I see examples of folks in our community making a go at it in small-scale, sustainable food production.

It is not only the massive reduction of income that keeps me from making the shift to a land-based cottage industry that is more in line with the goals of Emerald Earth and leads to much greater self-reliance as a community. Another factor is just the effort required. It's easy to go to town and come home with money. More than that, I would say, it's pleasant to do so. I live in a small ecovillage where we share two meals a day, have a dozen community projects going, and are blessed with the presence of kids needing attention. My drive to work is often the only quiet time I get all week, and being at work is the only time I'm not at risk of being distracted or interrupted by children, visitors with questions, or residents with needs or concerns.

Also, I get to make all the decisions about my business by myself, without asking anyone's opinions or permission, and without receiving feedback about how my choices affect each and every person living with me! Save the lecture about how important it is to work collectively, how much better decisions are when made in a group, and the pitfalls of our individualistic culture. I know and I agree—that's why I live in community. I also think it is important for individuals—adults and children alike—to have autonomy in some aspects of their lives. Running a land-based business on a property that you collectively steward with others is like navigating a ship through iceberg-laden waters.

Last year, my fellow resident Liz and I bought two cows, milking equipment, and miles of electric fencing. The goal—to use the cows to build topsoil and restore fertility to the native oak grasslands while producing delicious, nutrient-dense, raw dairy and grass-fed meat for us and to share with others who value that quality of food.

Everyone was supportive. Really, they were. It was hard to remember that, though, as we heard all the concerns—"Is that unsightly fencing going to stay there, where I like to go for a walk every day?" "The cows' hoof prints in the wet soil look like they're tearing up the land!" "It feels disrespectful that you keep having to leave meetings early to go milk." "I don't think you're paying the community enough rent considering the impact you're having on the land and the infrastructure" etc., etc. All valid concerns. All the sorts of concerns I would raise, myself, to someone else starting a business. But, as someone working her butt off trying to make a new project fly—or at least to be worth the money I'd put into it—it was difficult and discouraging.

All that for a project that if we wanted it as a business would make us less than minimum wage while not being quite exactly legal.

Which brings me to what I see as the biggest barrier many small, land-based businesses face—the prohibitive cost of time and money to comply with environmental, food safety, and other laws. I'm not a libertarian, and I fully support the spirit of most of these laws. Giant dairies—whose animals have numbers, not names—really should have a completely sterile environment and a $500,000 bottling facility. They shouldn't sell raw milk, and they do need to be inspected regularly. (I will not get into the debate over raw vs. pasteurized milk except to say that I would strongly warn against raw milk from an animal without a name, provided to you by a person you don't know.)

Some people use the "herd share" shared ownership model, where neighbors buy a "share" of the herd, and therefore get a share of the milk. Then they pay the farmer to care for and milk their animals for them. Everyone signs detailed contracts and understands what they're doing and the risks they are taking, drinking milk from an uncertified dairy. They are welcome to come visit their cows and watch the farmer milk them. They can even participate and muck out the barn! We'd love to do this. The herd has grown to three beautiful jerseys—Blossom, Honey, and Molasses. If any one of them becomes the slightest bit sick, I guarantee we'll notice.

And this is, as far as the feds are concerned, completely illegal. Last year, several herd share operations were busted throughout the state and the country. (Visit www.farmtoconsumer.org for more information.) This crackdown is ostensibly to protect public health, though it oddly seems to do more to protect corporate dairy profits. It is easier here in northern California to legally grow marijuana than it is to sell milk, cheese, pickles, or preserves—all of which require expensive equipment, commercial kitchens, and regular inspections. (Note: I recently learned of a new law passed in California which will make small cottage food production possible—though it excludes dairy.)

Other small business opportunities here are similarly legally dubious. Our work-

Tom makes firewood out of the byproduct of our restoration projects.

Cass brings kids from town to join ours for school in a teepee.

shops and classes, for example, involve us feeding folks. We do not have a commercial kitchen, or submit to regular inspections. Any plan to care for our forest through thinning will require an expensive and time-consuming Non-Industrial Timber Harvest Plan (NTHP) prepared by a licensed forester. Only then could we begin selling firewood or lumber legally. Capitalizing any of these ventures legally would take major investment or big debt, which is a part of the system we are trying to escape.

Liz took the plunge. She has taken a break from her eight-year-old acupuncture practice in town to fully engage with her passion. She is now working towards the greater vision, fully embodying the Permaculture principles of care for the land, care for the people, and return the surplus.

I chickened out. I still help milk the cows, and I deliver milk to friends in town on my way to work. But most days I sleep in 'til 6:30 or 7 a.m. (luxurious), spend more time with my family—not with them following me around as I do chores at the barn—and stress less about money.

And so I drive up and down the hill, freshly showered, back seat full of coolers of milk, with most of the dirt dug out from beneath my fingernails. I bridge the worlds, bringing some money back into our community, enjoying the drive and reviewing my decisions. For now, there is peace in the compromise. ❧

Abeja has lived at Emerald Earth with her family for the last six years, and she has lived in intentional community for the better part of the last 18 years. Folks still seem willing to put up with her.

Author and kraut: Since we don't have a commercial kitchen, the world may never know my kraut and kimchi.

The New Membership Challenge

We want (and need) more people here to help us really fulfill the vision we hold for this place. Unfortunately, the last several people in the membership process have struggled and ended up leaving Emerald Earth. Much discussion and reflection on why things haven't worked here has pointed at least one finger at money.

It has become much more difficult to make ends meet here since the financial crisis. Our monthly consumables cost per adult has risen from $180 to $265 in the last four years, while income earning potential in the area has stagnated or even dropped. Our current lack of strong cottage industries means that people arriving need to figure out their own source of income while still plugging into all the great unpaid work we have to do here.

Of course, debt only makes this situation even more tenuous, and, with the cost of education skyrocketing, it is a rare person under 35 who is not burdened with debt. Our current community financial system makes it nearly impossible for the majority of young, intelligent, hard working, educated folks to be able to live here without defaulting on loans.

"Living within our means" (i.e., eschewing debt) is a radical, revolutionary act in this day and age. Most kids today get trapped in the debt cycle as part of getting an "education," so the choice is often made before they can truly understand what that means. I have witnessed that, for many, debt can be a slippery slope. Once you already owe many thousands of dollars, why not add a few hundred more for the latest iPhone or festival?

Interpersonally, I see money—and how people use it—to be a major source of discord. Although we're not income-sharing, we are financially intertwined. Folks often arrive from the outside world with nice cars, clothes, smart phones, laptops, online shopping habits, etc. It can be especially difficult to avoid judgment when these new residents then find they can't meet their minimal financial obligations here due to debt, lack of planning or savings, and/or the difficulties of finding decent paying work in a rural economy. It can also be a big learning curve for folks from the dominant culture to integrate into our current culture of thrift store and craigslist shopping, mending and repairing, creative reuse, and making do with less stuff.

We come to this life with a vision of a new way. This begins with an escape from the parts of the culture that are holding us back, beating us down, keeping us separate, keeping us working jobs that don't serve us. But how do we disentangle ourselves? How do we help others in that process? Can we choose to leave some parts and keep others? How patient can we be with people who share our lives yet make different choices? Can we live our values without succumbing to the fears that are put on us to engage in the the current systems of health insurance, social security, and retirement investment?

The work we're doing is difficult and won't be completed in my lifetime. To keep going, I have to remind myself of the big picture—the future we envision for our children's children.

—A.H.

Jesus People USA member Trier washes dishes at the group's neighborhood soup kitchen in downtown Chicago during his evening dishwashing shift.

Communities That Serve Others . . .
and LOVE Doing It

BY DARIN FENGER

When the police burst into the dining hall at Jesus People USA one night in 1979, residents of the Chicago community had to swear they weren't running a soup kitchen without a permit.

They were just sharing their supper with a few friends—all 120 of them.

"We called it our dinner guest program," longtime resident Lyda Jackson said with pride. "But we never set out to start a soup kitchen—or a shelter! All of it really just came to us, just hap-

pened organically. People just started dropping folks on our doorstep."

Today Jesus People USA, a community born out of the so-called Jesus Freak movement, hasn't just carved a solid, storied living space out of a rough neighborhood up the street from Wrigley Field. The whopping 400-some residents have also built a small empire of programs tasked with giving love citywide to their brothers and sisters in need.

Just a few of their programs include a senior housing building, interim housing for families, a shelter for single women and after-school programs for kids offering everything from sports to tutoring. And yes, they still have the Dinner Guest Program, which feeds 150-200 people one day a week.

But don't expect residents to spout lofty reasons for giving. To Jackson their basic motivation is simple. They just want to put their Christian beliefs into honest action at a much-needed, basic level. That started when residents in the early days realized, when they were out in the streets taking their message to people, that it wasn't just souls that were hungry—bellies were, too. They realized that before a person's spiritual salvation could be had, their physical body had to be saved first.

Jackson explained how those early founders, who were originally looking to find themselves, ended up at their answer by beginning to look after everyone else.

"At that time we were young kids in the 1970s looking for deeper meaning in our lives and looking for ways to be living out our faith," Jackson said. "We have taken the commandments of Christ very seriously, especially where he talks about social justice issues. Where the Bible tells us to feed the hungry, clothe the naked, and visit the prisoner, I like to think that these are those people."

We never set out to start a soup kitchen—or a shelter. All of it really just came to us, just happened organically.

Just like Jesus People USA countless other intentional communities around the nation are actively—and often joyously—bucking that old stereotype of seclusion from the outside world. In these community's cases, they're very much a part of that world—healing it, nourishing it, and just plain cleaning it up.

Some communities got into service in other ways. Motivated by the desire to help, places like Magic, Inc. in Palo Alto, California, invented their entire way of life around the concept of residents giving not to just to each other, but to neighbors, strangers, and the planet itself.

David Schrom, a co-founder at Magic, said that the first residents made an honest assessment of their needs and realized that those requirements included a comfortable urban living space where benefits would include healthy food and modern appliances.

"We wanted to admit that those things are important to us," Schrom explained. "But we wanted them both for ourselves and others. We feel making a difference in our lives comes not just when we get these things ourselves, but in working to make them available for everybody."

Kathleen Monts (above) helps Shaquandra Barner and Adrianna Lincoln plant flowers outside Koinonia Community Outreach Center. Bonnie Tubbs, Jesus People USA's longtime neighbor, friend, and volunteer (below).

Such service isn't just dedication, though. It's also a path to happiness for Magic residents, with wholeness coming from that solid alignment between action and their truest values.

"The people who have come together as Magic share a common understanding that our satisfaction may depend more on others' enjoying things that are high on our lists of goods (for example, protection from violence at the hands of other people, nutritious food, clean air and water, decent housing)," he said, "than from our enjoying things lower on our lists (for example, fancy food, new clothing, expensive furnishings)."

That is why residents at Magic, since its founding in 1976, have taught life planning workshops and given seminars on topics ranging from science and value to habitat stewardship. They even have a major outreach program dedicated to awareness of sleep apnea. Residents also teach mediation, yoga, and swimming, as well as salvage thousands of fruit trees each year and teach young people how to plant them.

"Over time our central value has become loving, but ours is a process of continuing discovery," he said. "We act as we do and explain it when asked without pretending that it is 'good' or 'right' or that other ways are 'bad' or 'wrong' in any absolute sense. Rather, we're engaged in a process of trial and evaluation."

Magic residents have actually found that in addition to enriching residents' lives and bringing them closer together,

Service isn't just dedication, for Magic residents. It's also a path to happiness.

social service to their neighborhood and city also serves another vital function. It gives the entire community purpose, which immediately lends itself toward stability.

Schrom said that before he and his fellow founders opened Magic, they first sought out wisdom from existing communities. They read, asked questions of leaders around the nation, and studied communities that flourished and those that floundered. During that quest they came across important academic works from a Harvard professor who had studied the connection between social service and a community's chances for survival. The author was Dr. Rosabeth Moss Kanter and her book is *Commitment and Community: Communes and Utopias in Sociological Perspective.*

"She said that communities endure," Schrom said, "when they have a charismatic leader, are affiliated with a significant, long-standing tradition, or when they come up with some purpose that goes beyond the narrow confines of their membership. Since those other ways did not apply, our only choice was to become committed to something bigger than ourselves."

But don't expect Magic residents to confuse service with suffering. Schrom stressed how those who give are helping no one if they become trapped into thinking that giving only counts if

Magic member Heather Lukas (above) transports native plant species for transplanting around storm water retention basin. Jesus People USA notes that families with children represent the fastest-growing population of homeless people (below).

32

Taking a break from roofing and painting a neighbor's house, are (left to right) Koinonia member J. Reilly, "alternative spring break" students from the University of Virginia, and Arlen Daleske, a pastor on a service sabbatical at Koinonia.

it hurts. Schrom said he sees such a delusion as a serious threat to a community's most precious commodity—the human spirit.

"No martyrs here, please!" he said, chuckling softly. "The focus shouldn't just be for the good of the other, but for the common good. I'm part of this world, too, and it's not common good if I'm miserable and everyone's thinking 'Oh, what a great guy'."

"If you call us 'servants,' we take it as a compliment."

He added that a resident who's become misguided in their giving only stands the very real threat of burning themselves out, leaving a good cause and a community with one less caring heart.

Some intentional communities, though, aren't born out of struggle but there sure is struggle all the same. Koinonia, a small Christian farming community in Georgia, brought the races together in the early 1940s to live, work, pray, and strive for peace together. But that progressive way of life brought them some pretty harsh outcomes, including "boycotts, threats, sabotage, and bullets."

"Needless to say, Koinonia's antimilitarism, interracialism, and perceived 'Communism' got our southwest Georgia community in a lot of trouble for years —especially the mid-1960s," said Ann Karp, a current resident of the 20-person community. "Now, though we are no longer openly persecuted, these values are still central to our existence, and we still seek to serve each other and our neighbors. If you called us 'servants,' we'd take it as a compliment."

Today Koinonia's ministries include an outreach center serving everyone from youth to elders, a neighborhood program welcoming

people to join the community in "fellowship, work, service, prayer and study."

Koinonia also hosts a multitude of workshops and seminars, but its most famous offering is its Heart-to-Heart Home Repair Ministry, a program rooted in Koinonia's heritage as the birthplace of the now-famous Habitat for Humanity movement.

"Koinonia (was created) to follow Jesus' teachings as did the early churches described in the Acts of the Apostles. So service is central to our very existence. It is synonymous to being a good neighbor, which is one of the ways we live out our faith," Karp explained. "One of our founding members, Clarence Jordan, translated the gospels into the language and context of the Jim Crow South, where this farm was born. In the gospels, Clarence saw Jesus preaching and teaching three primary values: peace-

On the Web

Check out how Jesus People USA earn their much-needed funds by doing everything from making T-shirts for bands to recording their music: *www.jpusa.org*.

Learn more about Magic, Inc's unique philosophy, "value science": *www.ecomagic.org*.

Read how Koinonia's peace efforts have even entailed trips to the Middle East to learn more about the Israeli-Palestinian conflict: *koinoniapartners.org*.

—*D.F.*

try not to build walls," Karp said. "We know that our values are unfortunately not often embraced by the mainstream, but we try not to look at our situation as an us-them relationship."

To residents, that blend of giving and humility is a must. "From the beginning, Koinonians understood that we have no monopoly on knowledge and assistance." She shared the story of Clarence Johnson, who longed to help lift impoverished share-croppers from their cycle of debt but had no practical farming experience.

"But his neighbors did. So every morning, he'd climb onto the roof to see what they were doing. If they were plowing, he plowed. If they were planting, he planted. The sharing was

To Koinonia residents, that blend of giving and humility is a must.

mutual," she said. "When we remain aware of this dynamic, our service is much more humble and less in danger of becoming paternalistic."

The Koinonia resident stressed, too, that the gifts that come from service are truly not one-sided, either. "It fuels our own souls just as much as it helps others. Love is its own reward," she said.

Karp offered a few words of encouragement for intentional communities that don't incorporate service into their vision but are interested in the thought and just may be need a bit of encouragement.

"But even if you are initially skittish or uninspired by the prospect . . . I urge you to try it out. Start small. Give blood. Help out at the animal shelter," she said. "Join others' service pro-jects. You don't have to organize it yourself right in the beginning. It really can be addictive in the best sense of the word."

making, brotherhood (and sisterhood), and sharing according to need, not greed. Each of these values implies service."

The community's help is readily accepted by its neighbors, too, with the problem of intentional communities often being mis-understood or perceived as different or strange never being an issue—thanks to its service.

"Koinonia has been woven into the greater community since its inception. We have never sought to isolate ourselves, and we

Darin Fenger is a newspaper reporter living in southern Arizona.

Dawn Betenbough-Stoner, Kathleen Monts, and Victoria Higham (left) decorate the Koinonia Community Outreach Center. Clothing, books, and household items are available to local residents at Jesus People USA's Free Store (right).

FREE TO SERVE:
Notes from a Needs-Based Economy

By Chris Foraker

PHOTOS: ROSEMARY KIRINCIC

Throw It Against the Wall

Gandhi said something about life being an experiment. Experiments drive discovery. We gather the best information available, from books, stories, old people, previous experiments, and try something new in service to our thought dreams. "If my thought dreams could be seen they'd probably put my head in a guillotine." Dylan is right: thought dreams are dangerous. I'm not suggesting the following is very dangerous. It's actually quite ordinary—quite practical—just some observations from experiments with my own personal economy. But it does involve a process of dreaming, experimenting, and then observing—the stuff of creation. When we're creating (or co-creating) our world instead of accepting our world, we do become empowered. An empowered people can be dangerous to disempowering tendencies.

Wal-Mart came to Cottage Grove, Oregon, in '94, convinced the city council to change local zoning laws, and got the go-ahead to build a 108,000-square-foot warehouse store. In 2006, desiring expansion, Wal-Mart applied for another zoning change that would permit the construction of a 160,000-square-foot super center. Public hearings were called, yes/no buttons made, positions taken, and after six hours of testimony spanning three days, not much was surprising: well-dressed corporate lawyers; polarized atmosphere; emotional testimonies from those for and those against. It didn't take me long to put my anti-zoning-change sentiments into words which I delivered unemotionally in the fog of a waning fever. The hearing continued on at a boring pace, reaching a peak of monotony during the testimony of my fellow "againsts," whose collective voice became tortuously redundant and, I hate to say it, a bit self-indulgent.

By all conventional standards, I would be considered poor. I make between $200 and $400 a month, cook and heat my home with wood. I don't have running water. I'm not subsidized by wealthy parents. I live in a school bus.

The highlight of the public hearing for me was the testimony of the "fors." They helped exercise my internal sound receptors of empathy that, on occasion, allow me to pull out of the emotive mud of a polarized landscape and hear the concrete needs of "the other." What I heard coming from the "other side" was *I'm poor, whether from low-paying work or a fixed income, and I depend on low-cost goods to get by.* I could understand that. I can also, by all conventional standards, be considered poor. I make between $200 and $400 a month, heat my home and cook with wood, cut my costs when I can. I don't have running water. I'm not subsidized by wealthy parents. I live in a school bus.

An amusing tension arose. Here I am in much the same predicament as many from Clan Super Size, but instead of a desperate sense of scarcity and need for low-cost goods, I feel embraced by a world of hope and abundance. I feel secure while others feel vulnerable. I feel my needs are taken care of while others feel life is too expensive. What was the difference? This tension sparked observation.

Sharing the Surplus, Natural Giving, and the Community Context

Several months ago I was in need of space to park my bus. I wanted to be two miles outside of town, hopefully near the bike path with the potential to run an extension cord from a garage or outside outlet for electricity. The deadline for moving was past and I was starting to feel anxious to unburden my generous host. That Thursday during the Cottage Grove community's weekly social gathering—a mix of homegrown goods,

Exchanging goods and services: Chris stocking a woodshed for the winter.

Permaculture teaches us to share the surplus. It is not an act of charity where we create personal scarcity, but an act of sharing abundance. Sharing surplus can be as natural as giving away two-day-old baked goods destined for the compost, cuttings from a prolific raspberry patch, or squash from a bountiful harvest.

Permaculture teaches us to share the surplus. When we give away our surplus we can give it joyfully because, by definition, it is extra. It is not an act of charity where we create personal scarcity, but an act of sharing abundance. Sharing our surplus is as natural as giving away two-day-old baked goods destined for the compost, cuttings from a prolific raspberry patch, or squash from a bountiful harvest. When we receive a gift of surplus we can do so with dignity because we are confident we are not receiving more than can be comfortably given.

Marshall Rosenberg reminds us that giving to someone in the service of his or her need is satisfying. To illustrate this idea, he suggests recalling the last time we helped fulfill someone's need, thinking on it for a moment and noticing how we feel. This exercise, as he describes, always produces smiles and satisfaction the world around.

These ideas, though complete in their own right, are most satisfying when practiced in the context of community. Community can be understood as an intertwined latticework of people connected by a shared place and/or shared aspirations. Sharing our surplus and giving in the service of each others' needs works well in community because a community is a co-operative project that gives back. Each individual act of giving is seen in relation to and as a part of a greater whole. We don't give aimlessly in a fragmented social landscape but intentionally and joyfully in the service of a larger project. When we give within a community we also feel a sense of security—almost like a smart investment—because a community reciprocates and responds, based on its humanity, to our changing needs. A group of people is far more resourceful than one alone.

As winter approached I was in need of space. My host had a surplus of space and was in need of a certain type of skill,

tight spacing, and free locally made wine—I was introduced to a friend of a friend. After some friendly formalities, the subject of pursuit came up and she promptly offered me a space to park my bus: two miles outside of town, across from the bike path, near an electrical outlet. In return she asked for dry firewood and help with projects around the property.

This event was a first glimpse into a new way of looking at my personal economy. Over time, these same types of exchanges replayed over and over, generating a pattern. Slowly, words came to describe the pattern, not complete but like the first rough sketches of a living document. At its most fundamental level, it is members of a community sharing their surplus in the service of each others' needs. One might call it a needs-based economy.

which I was able to provide. Since living at the two-mile marker I have brought her dry firewood, helped paint a wall, remove a shelf, unclog a drain, clean junk from the yard, plant trees, and landscape. Going into spring our agreement has been fruitful and rewarding.

Living in a Needs-Based Economy

The willingness to exchange goods and services directly is essential to a needs-based economy because it changes the way we see the world. When we begin looking at our life as a mosaic of needs rather than a system of alienating labor and consumption, we transcend currency and put ourselves in touch with the abundance generated by an entire community.

It is common for someone to have the following thinking: "I need money so that I can buy the things I lack." This line of thinking is limiting and internally conflicting. It disconnects us from what we actually want and calls on a disempowering currency to mediate between us and our dreams. Instead, if we are able to envision our needs without currency, we open ourselves to the abundance of an entire community's surplus facilitated by people's tendency towards natural giving.

As winter arrived in Oregon, I soon discovered that living in the equivalent of a giant metal mailbox could be quite cold. Heat became an immediate priority. Wood was the natural choice, so I began my search for a stove and dry firewood, both of which I thought would be difficult to find as those more prepared began to calculate the heating power of their now dwindling reserves. On some of the colder mornings, as I lay under five layers of insulation watching my breath take shape in taunting cold-smoke signals above me, I considered the stoves listed for sale on craigslist and the pick-up trucks of firewood waiting and ready for delivery in downtown Cottage Grove. But, as things became desperate, a friend of a friend offered his old wood stove, just the right size, being stored in an abandoned trailer outside of town. No one was using it so he said I could have it for at least the winter. After heating with kiln-dried, quick-burning, industrial forestry waste for a while, I received a pickup truck load of dry hardwood and fir from a family of land stewards. So for most of the winter I stayed mostly warm.

By exchanging goods and services directly, we resist the tendency to do unfulfilling, alienating work. Robert Heilman de-

By exchanging goods and services directly, we resist the tendency to do unfulfilling, alienating work.

When home is the equivalent of a giant metal mailbox, heating became an immediate priority.
The solution: a loaner stove that was being stored in an abandoned trailer.

scribes life as an industrial logger in rural Oregon: "Alienation is an occupational disease, one that afflicts each of us when we sell our time for money. It brings a numbness of spirit that makes all sorts of horrible situations seem routine."

Instead, when we exchange directly, both giver and recipient benefit. In giving, we become connected to the act of creation, which is exhilarating. We once again become masters of our own time, liberated from the inevitable exploitation of a boss-wage system. Time becomes abundant and quality and joy can once again be incorporated into our work. Anything created by caring hands is infused with a uniqueness and life—easily seen in the difference between a modularized suburbia and a handmade home, or between a generic store-bought card with a "birthday check" enclosed, and a gift made with care and attention. In this way we become involved in each other's lives and allow parts of our internal and external landscapes to be shaped by our neighbors' artistic and clever natures. By exchanging directly we strengthen a culture of natural giving and shared surplus.

The thought of working for a wage to purchase a stove and cord of firewood now seems silly when faced with the possibilities available in a connected community. When the rains stop, I will gladly replace the amount of wood that was given to me or perhaps double the amount or triple, or perhaps I'll

(continued on p. 77)

FREE TO SERVE
(continued from p. 51)

just be helpful in some other way needed by the generous givers. When living within an economy based on joyful giving, two doesn't always equal two, but instead we are freed to give equal to the immense gratitude we feel upon receiving a gift from the heart.

Freed to Serve

I volunteer between eight and 20 hours a week for Cottage Grove's low-powered community radio station KSOW, often doing the small and mundane things that just need a body and half a brain to complete. I do this joyfully because it contributes to the larger community project, the radio station needs it, and I enjoy music. I have the time to volunteer largely because my needs are efficiently satisfied by an abundant community. The community has freed me to serve the community. I'm not strapped with the high everyday costs of my low-income brethren, but have fortunately marginalized, with the power of community, the need for US currency in my life. I work between 10 and 20 hours a week for bread money, most of which goes to food and the bus remodeling project. This abundance of time has allowed me to explore those things which make me feel most alive. And an economy that helps people come alive is an economy we desperately need. ❀

After spending almost two decades in the sprawling suburban sameness of an East Coast Jungle Gym, Chris Foraker escaped to the West where, fleeing the persistence of a quarter-life crisis, he found refuge in the foothills of the Cascade Mountains. That's where he currently resides. In a school bus.

psssssssssst!

Check out
communitybuzz.ic.org

Householding: Communal Living on a Small Scale

By Elizabeth Barrette

Householding involves the practice of intentional community in a single house with a group of people not all related to each other. Similar terms include "share-housing," "shared house," "sharehouse," and "group house." Householding offers most of the same advantages of companionship and economy as other forms of intentional community, but on a smaller scale that some people find more accessible. For many people, a shared house is their first experience with communal living—and in times of economic hardship, the frugality may cause people to try it who might not otherwise consider it.

Shared Houses

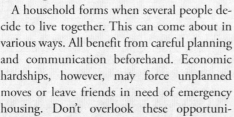

Householding is related to other types of intentional community. It is most closely connected to urban housing cooperatives, student co-ops, and cohousing. These models tend to feature concise living arrangements, often under a single roof.

A key feature of householding is the house itself. Shared houses typically evolve from large buildings such as farmhouses or Victorian mansions. They have multiple bathrooms and bedrooms, and generous common rooms and kitchens. It's possible, though more challenging, to share a smaller building. The number of bathrooms may prove more of a limiting factor than bedrooms in household population. Our house, Fieldhaven, is a large farmhouse with three current residents; it also hosts many events for our local like-minded community. Ravan Asteris, who also contributed input to this article, lives in a household of four adults over 40 (plus the landlord downstairs), five cats, and one dog in an 1890s Victorian house.

Shared houses may be short-term or long-term establishments. Those started by college students rarely last more than a year or few. During my college days I was a frequent guest, sometimes overnight, at one called Illinois Street House. Shared houses started by more settled adults can last for decades. Some even become famous in certain subcultures. For a while, I had friends at Lytheria in Milwaukee, Wisconsin: a modest mansion with individual bedrooms and large common rooms, and a waiting list for would-be residents. The Bhigg House in Winnipeg, Canada houses an assortment of musicians and other creative people; this household has collectively been invited to science fiction conventions as Guest of Honor.[1]

Forming a Household

A household forms when several people decide to live together. This can come about in various ways. All benefit from careful planning and communication beforehand. Economic hardships, however, may force unplanned moves or leave friends in need of emergency housing. Don't overlook these opportunities—it may be awkward, but helping each other through hard times is what community is all about.

The first approach to householding involves inviting people to move in with you.[2] This works well for a single person or couple with a large house, or at least a spare room; if your budget is tight, renters can help. It also benefits seniors, who often own a house but wish for more company. Pass the word among friends and family that you seek housemates. Check newspapers and bulletin boards in your area to find people who need living space. One trick for attracting housemates is to undercut the going rate for housing; another is to let people pay rent with barter instead of cash, especially if you aren't desperately broke. Ideally, seek people whose needs and interests mesh well with yours.

Stay alert for housing emergencies, a common dilemma in times of foreclosure and layoffs. Among the best ways to create a strong household is to provide living space for a friend who needs it on short notice. Start by offering temporary lodging, such as two to four weeks; use that time to test your compatibility. If you make a good fit, formalize a longer-term arrangement. If it doesn't work out, at least the emergency is taken care of and your friend has time to search for another place.

Economic hardships may force unplanned moves. Don't overlook these opportunities—helping each other through hard times is what community is all about.

The second approach to householding involves moving into someone else's place. This is easiest for a single person with minimal baggage, but may work for more people or possessions. First, use social networking (in person and/or online) to find opportunities. Perhaps some of your friends have a spare room they would like to rent out. Maybe someone has moved out early from a shared house and you could take over their lease.

If you can't find space with anyone you know, broaden your search. Local newspapers and bulletin boards may mention communal living opportunities. Check nearby colleges, because students frequently band together for housing and sometimes leave early. Finally, browse intentional community directories for shared houses or co-ops open to new members.[3]

The third approach to householding involves gathering a group of people who then rent or buy a place together. College students often do this, as one year's friends become next year's housemates. Experienced householders do it too. This way you can choose a building that meets your needs; you know how many bedrooms and bathrooms you need, and what other facilities or parameters are important. You also enter the household as equals; nobody has to move into somebody else's space or let someone into theirs.

On the downside, it can prove difficult to find a place that everyone likes. You may have to prioritize needs over desires, and that requires careful negotiation and honesty. Some towns have laws against unrelated people living together; even where it's legal, some landlords disapprove. These complications come up less often in college towns where students commonly rent houses together, or in cities or neighborhoods with old-fashioned "walkable" construction where duplex or triplex houses are common and amenities nearby.

Money Matters

In order to succeed, shared living requires a careful discussion of money, preferably at the beginning. Members must be absolutely clear about who contributes what, and when, and how. Ideally, one or more "anchor" members should have reliable income and credit, allowing the household the option of including others with different contributions.

Many groups choose to establish a household account, filled by rent or other arrangements, for paying common expenses such as utility bills and grocery shopping. This makes the bookkeeping easier; the household account can be managed by the person with the most financial or mathematical skill, and available for anyone to review upon request. Ravan Asteris adds, "In general, it is a good idea to start out with everyone making deposits, and then paying bills and buying common supplies out of the central account. This helps figure out what your real household expenses are. It's also good to overestimate the amount needed. Anything that isn't used in one month can be shunted to the savings, for months when the utilities spike or there are unexpected expenses (what do you mean, the neighbor kids broke a window?)." [4]

Some expenses tend to increase substantially as more people join a household. These include water, electricity, and phone bills. Your budget needs to account for this. The house phone may not increase much if everyone has their own cell phone, though.

Some expenses tend to stay the same, or increase only a little, as the household grows. These include heating/cooling, garbage, internet connection, and cable/satellite TV. Unless you choose to add more services, or add a lot of people, standard family packages usually cover these.

You can find many ways to save money by living together. [5] It is more economical to eat together than for everyone to buy their own food; budget more for communal groceries and take advantage of bulk pricing. Gather for activities, and you only have to light one or two rooms, not the whole house. Recycling, composting, and vermiculture reduce the need for garbage service. Share newspaper, magazine, and other subscriptions. Walking and biking save wear on the household car(s). Finally,

brainstorm money-saving ideas with your housemates.

Talking Points

Like other types of intentional community, a shared house benefits from fluent communication skills. Talk with your potential housemates before moving in together and discuss important points. It helps to have at least one person with facilitation and/or mediation experience. [6] Some households set formal meetings; others communicate more casually. Figure out what works for your group.

Practice verbal self-defense and avoid hostile language. [7] If you're new to householding, your job includes learning from more experienced members. If you've shared living space before, your job includes teaching communal skills to newcomers. Remember that under a single roof, you can't just walk away from conflicts—they come back to bite you later. Therefore, don't let disputes simmer until they boil over. Deal with them at once, gently if possible and firmly if necessary.

Explore the parameters for potential housemates. Do you want a like-minded group or a diverse group? Does it include employed, unemployed, self-employed, or part-time workers? Is the household open to children, college students, middle-aged adults, and/or seniors? Can you have pets and livestock, owned individually or collectively? What are people's dietary and other needs? What is the policy regarding tobacco, alcohol, and other substances? There are many ways to assemble a community, so read about some previous examples. [8]

Agree on a decision-making process for the household. Most groups prefer participatory options such as democratic, egalitarian, or consensus methods. If one person owns the house, however, that can lead to a more autocratic situation, which may or may not work for you.

Define what constitutes personal vs. public space. Which rooms are common rooms? What equipment is shared and what is private? What are the rules for using common space and equipment? How do housemates give each other necessary privacy? What balance between companionship and privacy do people want?

Discuss the distribution of chores and other responsibilities. Who does the cooking, cleaning, repairs, and other upkeep? Who has special skills or limitations? Express thanks for tasks completed; everyone enjoys being appreciated. Also compare "mess quotient," one of the commonest reasons for domestic friction that people rarely consider. How messy or tidy should public spaces be? What about individual bedrooms or other private places? Generally, divide chores based on ability and interest, so that nobody has to do things that they hate, that they do poorly, or that aggravate their health issues. Two types of task

> *Remember that under a single roof, you can't just walk away from conflicts—they come back to bite you later.*

should be shared by all: those that everyone dislikes, and those that everyone enjoys.

Compare people's wake/sleep schedules and work/home schedules. Discuss your tastes in music, conversation, and other aspects of noise level. Do you want to establish specific quiet times or revel times? Could you use the physical layout of the house to separate noisy activities from peaceful ones? Here at Fieldhaven, we've found that having people on different sleep schedules poses no serious problems—as long as the day sleeper is upstairs, not downstairs near the door that makes a racket every time it opens or closes.

Explore your thoughts regarding guests. Can housemates bring home anyone they want, at any time? Do guests need to be known to other housemates? Are visits to be planned or spontaneous? May guests spend the night in a housemate's room, or in common space such as a couch? Households that frequently host overnight guests may want to invest in a futon or hide-a-bed sofa. Fieldhaven has two, a full-size couch and a loveseat, because we have several out-of-state friends who need crash space when visiting.

Finally, consider the issue of trust. Ravan Asteris explains, "If A hands B $20 to go to the store and get XXX, will they actually get it or return the money? If C falls off a ladder, will D call 911, and not just leave the house? You can be friends with people, but not trust them enough to live with them. Everyone has their faults and foibles, but if those faults are in the trustworthiness area, and are outside the bounds of what can be coped with by the rest of the household, the household will break down very quickly and/or expel the person that they can't trust. This doesn't mean that they have to be always honest, always perfect accountants, always 'clean,' or whatever, but they have to keep the trust of the household." [9]

Homemaking

Although economic and other practical reasons may cause people to share a dwelling, it takes more to create a thriving and cohesive household. For that you need homemaking skills, the knowledge and practices that merge individuals into a group. Pay attention to the group dynamics, nurture the collective identity, and generally encourage housemates to cooperate on projects. Create customs and traditions that define your household as a social unit.

Food provides comfort as well as nourishment. If possible, prepare meals collectively and eat together.[10] Team up for canning or freezing fruits and vegetables for later use. Take advantage of crock pots and other methods that fill the house with delicious smells for hours before a meal. Share recipes by creat-

ing a cookbook of household favorites. Exchange the news from each other's successes and challenges of the day over supper.

Spend leisure time together. Find out who enjoys the same crafts or hobbies, and who would like to learn new ones from someone else. Encourage "lapwork" activities such as sewing, knitting, or woodcarving that people can do while conversing. Share board, card, roleplaying, or physical games once or twice a month.[11] Movie nights are popular. Also consider music nights if your housemates sing or play instruments.

Finally, name your household. While not obligatory, a name helps make it real and memorable. It also gives you an easy way to talk about your shared house and your collective housemates. You might choose a name inspired by the house or yard, location, favorite literature, mythology, or other characteristics. It should sound interesting and welcoming. Above all, it should capture the spirit of the place and the people who call it home.

This is your dream. Give it roots—and then give it wings. ✢

Elizabeth Barrette writes nonfiction, fiction, and poetry in the fields of alternative spirituality, speculative fiction, and gender studies. She supports the growth of community in diverse forms and is active in local organizations. Her favorite activities include gardening for wildlife and public speaking at Pagan events and science fiction conventions. Visit her blog at gaiatribe.geekuniversalis.com.

1. "Minicon 30 Fan Guests of Honor: BHIGG HOUSE" by Steve Glennon, reference taken 3/25/09.
www.mnstf.org/minicon/minicon30/bhigg-house.html
2. "How to Find a Housemate or Roommate" by Pondripples, eHow, reference taken 3/26/09.
www.ehow.com/how_4730509_housemate-roomate.html
3. *Communities Directory, 2007: A Comprehensive Guide to Intentional Communities and Cooperative Living* by Fellowship for Intentional Community. Fellowship for Intentional Community, 2007.
4. "Money Talks" by Ravan Asteris, LiveJournal Community Householding, 2/26/09.
community.livejournal.com/householding/1328.html
5. "Household Budget Tips" by Always Frugal, 2004-2009.
www.alwaysfrugal.com/
6. "Tree Bressen's Group Facilitation Site" by Tree Bressen, 2008-2009.
treegroup.info/
7. *The Gentle Art of Verbal Self-Defense* (Revised Edition) by Suzette Haden Elgin. Fall River Press, 2009.
8. *Shared Visions, Shared Lives: Communal Living Around the Globe* by Bill Metcalf. Findhorn Press, 1996.
9. "Essentials: Trust" by Ravan Asteris, LiveJournal Community Householding, 2/22/09.
community.livejournal.com/householding/772.html
10. *Cooking Time Is Family Time: Cooking Together, Eating Together, and Spending Time Together* by Lynn Fredericks. William Morrow & Co., 1999.
11. "Team Builders, Ice Breakers, Songs, Name Games and Other Fun Games" by Resident Assistant, 1998-2008.
http://www.residentassistant.com/games/

> *Although economic and other practical reasons may cause people to share a dwelling, it takes more to create a thriving and cohesive household.*

Balancing Act:
How Much Are You Willing to Share?

By Janel Healy

I think it's safe to say that you are an idealistic person. As a supporter of Com-MUNITIES, you've probably thought long and hard about how to live a life that's more just—and just better—and it looks like you've come to the conclusion that living communally may be the answer.

But how "communal" do you have to get before you're truly living according to the ideals of Right Livelihood?

Ask this question to someone who's living in an income-sharing community, and the answer may sound a bit extreme. At neighboring egalitarian communities Twin Oaks and Acorn, located in rural central Virginia, all the "big stuff" is cooperatively owned—from houses and cars to bank accounts and businesses. For some of these communes' members, environmental concerns are motivation enough to share almost everything. Valerie, who's been living at Twin Oaks for two decades, believes, "Anyone who wanted to be living according to Right Livelihood would share cars. It's much less of a footprint on the earth." For others, such as Tom from Twin Oaks, it's all about the worker-owned businesses. "Income sharing *itself* is right livelihood," he asserts. "We don't have an ownership class, so we're not working hard to make others rich. Here, workers are managers—not just tools for producing capital."

When it comes to supporting good causes, income sharing is a testament to "power in numbers." If your economic unit is two people, your chief concern may be keeping your "unit" afloat financially. You may not have much leeway in terms of choosing a job that fits in with your values, nor time to volunteer or money to donate. But when your economic unit is say, 25 people (Acorn's current population), the group has more resources, time, and skills to put towards endeavors its members believe in. And when your economic unit is nearly 100...well, take it from Twin Oaks—you can pool your resources so efficiently as to live on about $5,000 per person per year. Those who are sick, elderly, or otherwise unable to fully pull their weight can be supported

by the dozens of members who can, and the group has even more freedom to decide how to invest its money, time, and resources positively.

However, even though income sharing can be a successful way to band together to provide a secure and moral livelihood for a group, it's not easy. In fact, as a relatively new member, I must say that adjusting to life at Twin Oaks is still an ongoing challenge. It's been difficult getting used to having little financial autonomy. I feel frustrated that public possessions at Twin Oaks can get trashed easily—people tend to forget about the personal responsibility that comes with collective ownership. And I can't help but feel uneasy that folks who aren't working as efficiently as they could be are getting the same amount of "labor credits" as those who are.

I also sometimes find myself wondering what more I could be doing for the world. Am I living as closely to the notion of Right Livelihood at Twin Oaks as I could be? How far out does one have to reach in order to be living responsibly?

After speaking with several members of both Acorn and Twin Oaks in preparation for this article, though, I've come to realize that living in an income-sharing community as well as living by the guidelines of Right Livelihood are delicate balancing acts. There's no manual specifying how to embody Right Livelihood in every situation, nor is there a manual on how to thrive within the challenging environment of an income-sharing community (although Twin Oaks *does* have a 200-page book of community policies). I'm starting to understand that it's all about perspective, and about finding satisfaction, not guilt, in challenging yourself to do the best you can do. And living in an

Tom, who runs Twin Oaks' organic cut flowers business, tending to seedlings that will eventually become gorgeous flowers to sell at local farmers' markets.

Sarah Rice

intentional community—especially in an income-sharing community, where collectivism can allow for a greater expression of values—provides the challenge to raise the bar in terms of responsible living.

For instance, because Acorn is a consensus-based community with biweekly meetings, its culture of discussing all group decisions face to face encourages members to think deeply about the choices they make. According to River, who's been a Virginia communard for the past 25 years, this is especially true with purchases. "Modern society is based on impulse buying," he explains. "If I were living on my own, I might go to the grocery store and pick up ramen noodles for dinner without thinking much about it." But when you're sharing your meals with a group, he says, you have to talk to each other about what kind of food to purchase and eat. "It forces you to question these things. There's a discussion about, 'What's the best way to do this, not just for personal health but also for the earth?'"

At Twin Oaks, you don't have to think very hard at all about using less fuel or electricity to have a lighter impact on the land. It's just a part of everyday life because of the community's culture of home and car sharing. "The way we live and share everything is more ecological, but it's easy for us to make those choices," Valerie says. "Mainstream society is not set up to make those choices. Often there are other priorities."

But does Twin Oaks adequately challenge its members to do service outside of the intentional communities movement? In a classic case of poor perspective, I've recently felt discouraged at the thought that Twin Oaks doesn't. I thought that the community's lack of emphasis on serving those in need was keeping me from emphasizing it in my own life. However, in talking to Ira, who moved to Twin Oaks in 1985 and then became a founding member of Acorn in 1993, I realized it's my own fault that I haven't been contributing to good causes outside of the communities movement since I've lived at Twin Oaks.

Ira and Andros of Acorn Community watering and working with the community's roselle plants (to be used eventually for tea leaves).

Janel Healy

A culture of discussing all group decisions face to face encourages members to think deeply about the choices they make.

All I have to do is go out and do it.

"When I lived at Twin Oaks, I'd take different crews of people to local farms to harvest peaches and other stuff the community didn't grow," Ira told me. "I didn't do it for labor credits, at least at first. I'm just into supporting local farmers, so that they can support their families. This makes it more likely that they will continue farming using organic principles."

Because Ira has energy and people organizational skills, she was able to tap the vast pool of skills and labor available to her at Twin Oaks when she wanted to start a project or embark on a service mission. If she had been living outside of community, it could have been much harder for her to rally people together to volunteer their time and money to support a cause. "It's all about having enough energy to work on projects because it's the right thing to do and not necessarily because it'll make money or fulfill your labor quota," Ira imparts. "Anywhere you live, living according to the ideals of Right Livelihood takes a lot of energy. It might take even more energy outside of community."

Now, Ira is constantly able to tap into her enthusiasm for changing the world through local agriculture thanks to Acorn's heirloom seed business, Southern Exposure Seed Exchange (SESE). Acorn, with sheer good luck on its side, had the option of purchasing SESE at a time when the community was looking for an ethical, organic agriculture-related business to sustain itself. "We realized that good seed is the foundation of sustainable agriculture," says Ira, "and so SESE was like putting on a pair of shoes that was just right."

Down the road at Twin Oaks, the major community businesses are Twin Oaks Tofu and Twin Oaks Hammocks. For some Oakers, producing hammocks—leisure products made with synthetic rope—doesn't quite match up with their idea of Right Livelihood. However, as Acorn's Andros observes, "Hammocks sustained Twin Oaks long enough for the community to be able to survive. Twin Oaks has since reinvested that money into ventures that are arguably more righteous."

Author hauling clean laundry from Twin Oaks' main laundry facility back to her building: "Even the way we do laundry here at the Twin Oaks Community is an example of Right Livelihood (in an ecological sense). We have only three washing machines for almost 100 people, and whenever it's sunny, a lot of us hang clothes out to dry instead of using a power-intensive dryer."

Income-sharing communities can be challenging places to live, but they provide an immense array of opportunities for doing good.

Andros, who's been living at Acorn for the past three and a half years, has a point. The hammock business, although not necessarily "sustainability"-focused, allowed Twin Oaks to simply exist. As Twin Oaks' first business, it gave a community of resource sharing and egalitarianism a chance to put down roots. Now, Twin Oaks has a variety of businesses that focus on sustainability through supporting local and/or organic agriculture—the community grows organic seeds for SESE and other seed companies; buys local, organic, and non-GMO soybeans for its tofu; and grows and sells organic cut flowers at nearby farmers' markets.

Plus, as Ira pointed out, it's important for an income-sharing community to have many different jobs that are suited to various people and skills. "The hammock business is useful for Twin Oaks because almost anyone can learn [hammock-making] quickly and can use it to contribute to the group," she explains. "Making healthy vegan tofu seems more ethical to a lot of Oakers, but the work isn't suited to as many people. It's important to have a culture where a large amount of people can contribute through a wide range of jobs."

Talk about a lesson in perspective.

Another Right Livelihood issue with which my fellow communards grapple is how much to allow our community businesses to grow. To Ira, the ability to have enough money to purchase local and/or organic food to supplement what Acorn can grow is extremely important. She remembers that she thought she'd "died and gone to heaven" the day Acorn, thanks to SESE, could finally afford to purchase organic coffee. "Right livelihood entails living a life that isn't all fancy but does allow you to buy the things you think are right," says Ira. "We grow some of our own things, but we also want to buy food from organic and sustainable sources." Twin Oaks' Tom might agree. "Right livelihood is not just what you do to make money—it's what you do with the money," he told me.

On the other hand, Pam, manager of the prolific Twin Oaks garden for the past 15 years, is dubious of the idea of using money to vote for change. She'd rather her community simply be the change by becoming even more self-sufficient. "Do we want to focus on how much to earn and what to spend it on, or do we want to reduce our

dependence on the cash economy?," she ponders. "The latter is my preference."

From Pam's perspective, how can anyone—or any community—really know that what they're buying is coming from an ethical source? A business could sell a product that it claims to be organic, but if the business has, say, a hierarchical power structure and poor working conditions, there isn't an intention of Right Livelihood behind the product. In this global economy, as Andros put it, there could be "an element of exploitation and unsustainability" in every financial transaction.

But should our communities stop buying things altogether? It doesn't seem realistic (nor good for morale)—not when so many people deeply enjoy or have even come to feel they need some of the comforts of modern life. The answer must therefore lie somewhere between dependence and complete independence when it comes to the cash economy. It's just another balancing act.

Although diverse opinions and perspectives of members can be stressful to those living in community—especially to those living in tightly knit income-sharing communities—it may actually be that this diversity keeps a community centered. Personally, I'm learning to take in many perspectives in order to have a balanced diet of food for thought. As River recommends, "Holding conflicting ideas in your head at once seems to be the best way to be flexible." I'm learning to embrace both the frustrating and the positive—income-sharing communities can be challenging places to live, but they provide an immense array of opportunities for doing good. Acknowledging how my community could do better in terms of Right Livelihood is necessary for "raising the bar" for the group and for myself, but it's also important to appreciate the ways in which my community does allow me to live according to my values.

Living in an income-sharing community is not the only way to lead a life according to the ideals of Right Livelihood, of course. Worker-owned cooperatives often share the ideals of Right Livelihood that Twin Oaks and Acorn hold so dear, as do other intentional communities that don't pool their earnings. "A lot of different communities and co-ops are part of the solution to a more equitable world," Ira explains. "It's not just one size fits all!" But for some people, income sharing is the perfect values match. "Most communities choose to do certain things together, but the more you do as a group, the more powerful it is," says River. "The ability to share resources creates something bigger than myself. I think that's a common human desire—to come together with other people to create something bigger."

When I think about the long term, I'm not yet sure where my life will fall along the spectrum of Right Livelihood lifestyles. I want to challenge myself to live as morally as possible, and although income-sharing communities are one great way to do that, I know there are other options. But for now, I'm appreciating the wonderfully just nature of sharing. I'm grateful to be living in a place where egalitarianism discourages the greed that seems to be plaguing much of the world. Tom puts it best: "For the few to have much, the many must have little. But at Twin Oaks, everyone *has*." If that's not Right Livelihood, I don't know what is.

For more information about secular income-sharing communities, visit the Federation of Egalitarian Communities online at www.thefec.org.

Janel Healy, a California native, has been living at the Twin Oaks Community in Louisa, Virginia for the past year. An avid sculptor of words, Janel has most recently written for Survive and Thrive TV, Positive Impact Magazine, *and the previous issue of* Communities. *Janel also spends her time making tofu, caring for chickens, and marketing for the 2011 Twin Oaks Communities Conference. One of her goals is to spread knowledge about the intentional communities movement to people across the country.*

More Perspectives from Acorn

I have lived at Acorn for only seven months, but it feels right to me to live communally. I feel good about sharing cars and farming equipment. If we were living separately in mainstream society, we would be using 25 cars, 25 washing machines, 25 toasters, 25 blenders; the list goes on and on. Now we share five cars, two washing machines, one toaster, one blender, etc. In my old apartment building in New Jersey, there was no recycling program. Acorn has a compost pile and recycles everything that can possibly be recycled. Surplus clothes go to Goodwill and surplus vegetables go to a local food bank. It makes me feel good to hang the laundry outside to dry, that our main residence only has one air conditioner (to store the seeds for our business), and that I haven't driven a car in seven months. I love growing and eating our own fruit and vegetables, knowing that they were not touched by pesticides and that they were handpicked by myself or people I know.

I don't miss my $60,000 a year job. Ultimately, it is not about money. To me, it's about living right.

I finally found a place to live where I feel good about myself and the impact I have on the earth. Before I started living at Acorn, I felt lonely, angry, scared, and unappreciated. Now I feel support, friendship, love, and appreciation. Life is not perfect, but it sure feels a hellofalot better.

—**Jacqueline Langeveld**
Acorn Community

I've been in community for most of the past eight years, and I've been at Acorn for most of the past two years. Since coming to community, I've been grateful for the chance to live close to the earth and in relative harmony with it, tending gardens, drying herbs, etc., and for the chance to live with people who understand my desire to do these things. I don't feel I make sacrifices for sustainability; I feel I've escaped the mainstream pressure to consume. I've never wanted my own car, my own house, my own computer, or the most fashionable clothes. In community, that doesn't make me weird. However, some people at Acorn might miss those things, the same way I sometimes wish I could build up more of a fund for travel or for something like retirement.

At Acorn, and in large part thanks to SESE, we don't just try to reduce our own ecological footprint; we also contribute to the sustainability endeavors of many others. We sell seed to gardeners and small farmers. We answer customers' questions about gardening, host seed swaps, and give workshops. We cooperate with other similar seed companies. Together, we help keep heirloom varieties alive. I send out donations of seeds to school gardens, community gardens, and the like. When we plant too much of something for ourselves, I pack up the extra for the local food bank. The same goes for when we plant, say, melons according to how much seed we need, but can't eat all the fruit. When students at nearby colleges move out and throw away huge amounts of perfectly good stuff, I ask myself how we can organize better salvage operations, responding to authorities' concerns, and perhaps giving what we can't use to charity. All in all, I am so glad I don't have to sell my time to earn a salary. The work I do here is not for money, but for the benefit of the community, society, the earth, and my own growth.

Though Acorn and Twin Oaks are egalitarian communities, we couldn't claim to be perfectly fair, or to be perfectly sustainable, or to have worked out all our differences. One of the difficulties with adjusting to life in an income-sharing community can be the level of trust our fellow communards expect of us. I sometimes get frustrated trying to reduce the amounts of food, electricity, and work time that we waste. Yet in the larger scheme of things, I trust that Acorners will continue to do the work that ensures that our basic needs will be met. I trust that if one of us gets very ill, that person will be taken care of. I trust that we will continue to listen to one another when making hard decisions.

—**Irena Hollowell**
Acorn Community

The Values of Shared Ownership

By Tim Miller

When the call for articles for this issue came out, I immediately thought that the editor would get plenty of essays dealing with personal relationships, solving problems, and other things having to do with human interaction. No one who has lived in community, I suspect, could fail to have learned many things about people and the way they relate to each other, and I'm no exception. Many years after leaving my community, however, the lesson that sticks with me most prominently is a rather material one: I learned about shared ownership and its practical benefits.

Sharing is not uncommon at the micro level; many a homeowner, for example, buys and shares tools with neighbors. My sister and her partner own a car-top carrier with another couple, and they pass it back and forth as one family or the other goes on a trip. My neighborhood has an appliance dolly that any of several dozen people can use at moving time. Most of us know of shared ownership at that level.

But real estate? That's a different matter, or at least it seems to be today.

I lived in a small community (seven or fewer members most of the time) whose house and land were owned, initially, by five individuals. We never could have bought the property in the first place had we relied on individual resources—rather meager savings, plus minimal income from public-service jobs. Working together, however, we pooled what money we had, found an outside supporter who bought a large share without intending to live on the property, took out a loan, signed the papers, and moved in. It never really occurred to any of us that was we were doing was dangerous, or even unusual. That was in the 1970s, and shared ownership didn't seem all that unusual in those days of idealism and rural romanticism—it was just what a lot of people were doing.

After about three years some owners left, and others came on board, with the reconstituted group of owners, plus some non-owner members, still living together. Although all of the owners moved out over time, and the house thus became a rental (again, from time to time, to a group), we continued to own the property jointly and use it in various ways for more than 30 years. Finally, however, with the inevitable changes that come over time, three of the four owners decided it was time to sell. I was the only one who wanted to keep the place.

Although by then I had a job and an income, I couldn't afford to buy them all out. So I began searching for new partners. But I quickly learned that carefree hippie days were long past. The people who had some interest in living in the country and/or owning rural property all seemed scared stiff of joint ownership. Some proposed to buy the house and part of the land—an unacceptable arrangement, because the layout of the land and the various amenities of the place didn't fit neatly into proper parcels. The things I liked best about the place were scattered here and there over many acres.

Finally it was time to fish or cut bait. The real estate market had hit bottom, but the others wanted to go ahead and get it over with. So I flung the net one last time, sending a message to everyone I could think of, searching one last time for interest in shared ownership. And from those hundreds of people I got one expression of interest. It all went forward from there, and today we are joint owners.

The reason why my new partners weren't scared with joint ownership is that they had experience with it. One of the new couple was a pilot who had wanted an airplane but couldn't afford one, so bought a new airplane jointly with another pilot. That had all worked out well, and she was ready to try again. A few weeks later we were signed, sealed, and delivered.

So I now have access to many mostly wild acres of land, a nice swimming hole, and a couple of structures that provide shelter in the sometimes-harsh climate of the central Midwest.

(continued on p. 73)

THE VALUES
OF SHARED OWNERSHIP

(continued from p. 35)

I can walk all over the place and enjoy the wildlife and the solitude. And my partners have just what I do—ownership of and access to a place they could not have afforded by themselves.

Do we ever have conflicts? Not very many, actually. Everyone involved is fairly reasonable, and we have a live-and-let-live attitude about what we do on the land. I look forward to many more years of having a place to go unwind, and if another sensible opportunity for group ownership comes my way, I'll consider it seriously. That's my greatest takeaway from my years in community. I don't think of myself as a relentless materialist, but I'm pretty convinced that cooperation can lead to practical material outcomes: if you share you can have more. ❧

Tim Miller teaches in the Department of Religious Studies at the University of Kansas and is a historian of American intentional communities. His books include The Quest for Utopia in Twentieth-Century America *and* The 60s Communes: Hippies and Beyond, *both published by Syracuse University Press, and* The Encyclopedic Guide to American Intentional Communities, *published in 2013 by Richard Couper Press.*

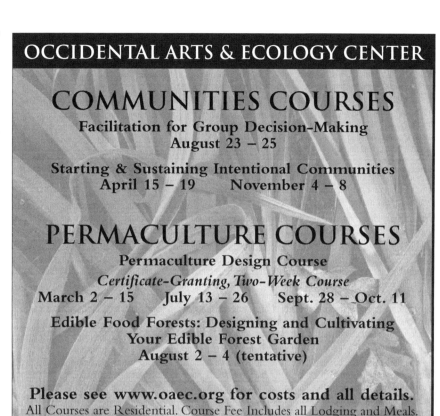

THE QUEST FOR COMMUNITY

JENNIFER MORRELL

As soon as i discovered my first intentional community at the age of nineteen, i knew i wanted to live that way. Sharing resources to lighten our load on the planet. Building a life together based on trust and cooperation instead of competition. Living out our ideals, right? My path was clear.

When i finished school, i set out with a sweetheart on what we called "The Quest for Community." We spent a year touring communities around the country, getting more clear with each visit on what we were looking for. Finally we settled down at Acorn Community in Virginia, a recent spin-off from the venerable Twin Oaks commune. It was the fall of 1994.

It was an exciting time to be at Acorn. The community doubled in population that fall, as a new residence was just on the edge of completion. The newcomers were full of verve and fresh ideas; old-timers wryly dubbed the season "the October Revolution," but supported us in trying things out. We had all the ups and downs of any group, and in the process created bonds that have kept many of us in contact with each other—even though no one who joined Acorn during that era remains there today.

A PERSONAL JOURNEY INTO THE GREY ZONE

i find myself in a grey zone between intentional community and a typical American lifestyle.

I dove into community life full force, and furthermore, into the communities movement. Ira Wallace, already a long-time communitarian by then, mentored me into involvement with both the Federation of Egalitarian Communities (FEC) and the Fellowship for Intentional Community (FIC). My friends in college had kindly put up with years of me singing the praises of community life from the outside. Now i was a joyous zealot from the inside. At home i proudly ran our outreach programs, leading tours and corresponding with hundreds of potential visitors. Traveling to communities movement meetings, i used the opportunity to tell everyone i met on trains and buses about the virtues of both my community and intentional communities in general.

My identity was so tied up in being a member of Acorn that any question a stranger asked me naturally led down that road:

"Where do you live?"

"At a communal farm in Virginia."

"What kind of work do you do?"

"Oh, lots of different kinds. Mostly i run the outreach programs for the commune i live at."

"Do you have children?"

"I really enjoy community living because it gives me the opportunity to be around kids without taking on all the responsibility of having my own."

You get the idea.

Having my identity so wrapped up in my community home also meant that even when i wasn't feeling satisfied there anymore, it took a long time before i'd consider living anywhere else. But in the spring of 1999, i left Acorn to move in with a polyamorous family in a small town on the Oregon coast. We were in love, something i'd been sorely missing the last few years at Acorn, and it was a chance to pursue another long-held dream.

I had come to realize that who i was was more than my Acorn membership. I promised myself that i would never again allow any one facet of my identity to keep me from fully exploring life.

From Acorn to Walnut

New relationships don't always work out, and a few short months later i was abruptly searching for a new home. I needed somewhere to go, fast. Having just moved all my stuff to Oregon, i couldn't see heading back east. There was an opening at an intentional community in Eugene, one that i had been impressed with back on the original "Quest for Community" road tour. A friend there helped clear the way, and i moved into Du-má, a group of people sharing a big, beautiful house, flourishing garden, common dinners, and clear values. After my bumpy try at life on the "outside," i felt so relieved to be back in community!

---

i promised myself that i would never again allow any one facet of my identity to keep me from fully exploring life.

After renting there for about a year, i left in the summer of 2000 to help found Walnut St. Co-op, in a lovely old home on the east side of town, with other folks who shared my passions for group process, facilitation, and social change. While dealing with significant turnover in the early years, we nevertheless managed to form a core group and, in 2003, buy our house from the resident who had bought it for us to begin with, starting our own community revolving loan fund for the purpose *(see "Our Community Revolving Loan Fund" in Communities #128, Fall 2005).*

In that intense year, when the fate of the home we loved rested upon the core group's ability to fulfill major legal and financial obligations (incorporation, raising hundreds of thousands of dollars in loans and donations, and finding some insurance company that would sell property coverage to a co-op), i threw myself into the tasks of the community as much as i ever had at Acorn. I was utterly dedicated to the cause of ensuring our survival, even while working

Opposite: Residents Alex, Tree, Erik, and Jen together in the heart of their shared house—the kitchen. Left: Tree's new home isn't officially a community, but it is enriched by the many friends who come to visit. Guest Chris Howell helps out by digging a garden bed.

three other part-time jobs. My housemates (both then and later) would occasionally complain of my tendency to speak as if i had "the" truth, not recognizing that the same trait which understandably annoyed them—that of believing in my own truth and vision of our community so strongly— was also making it possible for me to raise thousands of dollars on our behalf, to put a vision into the world and

sibly accept the mind-boggling inefficiencies of cooking for just one or two people every single night? Instead, i find myself in a grey zone between intentional community and a typical American lifestyle.

As we started to think seriously about finding a new place to live, i lobbied Alex—unsuccessfully, as it turned out—to buy a parcel of land across the street from a cohousing

---

For the first time in seven years, house meetings are no longer a weekly fixture on my calendar.

---

make it real. We met our deadlines and made it through, and Walnut St. Co-op continues in Eugene today.

However . . . i'm not living there. As with leaving Acorn, it took months of consideration before i was willing to make the move, in 2007, from Walnut St. to a much more private life. Everyone who lived at Walnut in those months has their own story of what happened—but anyway, my partner Alex and i chose to leave. I was afraid i would feel lonely and isolated in mainstream life. And who could pos-

community that was just a few months shy of move-in. "Think of it!" i said. "We'll have all the advantages of community life: built-in friends, someone to feed the cat while we're away, and those all-important common dinners. Unlike the standard condo uniformity at most cohousing communities, you'll be able to do whatever you want with the property, you can build and garden to your heart's content. And with our extra land, we'll be able to offer the cohousing residents benefits they can't get at home, like

51

additional space for storage or offices, or an invitation to kick back around a campfire."

Unfortunately, the cohousing community i was so excited about co-locating with wasn't in Eugene. Having moved here a year and a half earlier to pursue a relationship with me, Alex was finally starting to feel settled, with friends and activities in the neighborhood and his brother's family across the street. He searched his soul, and with deep sincerity, told me he couldn't pull up stakes to start over again someplace else, no matter how attractive the opportunity.

Unhappy with the outcome, but committed to remaining together, i put it to him to help generate more options for us closer to home. Alex looked and looked and came up with a house three blocks from the co-op, for sale at an unusually low

price due to black mold infestation and other issues. With an odd layout upstairs that required walking through two bedrooms in order to get to the bathroom, it looked entirely unsuitable for community life to me, but all his instincts were telling him to go for it, and so, trusting him, i reluctantly went along.

Is This Community or Not?

As i write this article, i sit at a desk in our new home, which i am pleased to report is now mold-free. (Alex basically tore out and rebuilt every part of the house that showed signs of infestation.) In

Opposite: Walnut St. Co-op in 2007. Top left: Whenever the Orchard St. household is wondering whose fault something is, they spin the "Wheel of Blame." The group is convinced that every community needs one. Top right: The new house needs a lot of work. Here, Alex paints the front room.

addition to Alex and me, his best friend Jen and her partner Erik live here, along with our four-legged companions. The other couple has the upstairs as bedroom and art studio, while Alex and i have a bedroom downstairs and, soon, a twenty foot yurt. We all share use of the living room, kitchen, and outdoors.

Unlike Walnut St., with its carefully constructed co-op ownership, Alex owns this house. The four of us have all been working hard fixing the place up. Lately i've been doing our food shopping, while another housemate tends the compost and gardens, another one has created an outdoor workshop area in the back, one person pays the bills, and so on: roles we've fallen into with little or no discussion. For the first time in seven years, house meetings are no longer a weekly fixture on my calendar—in fact, we haven't had *one*. However, we do have common dinners cooked by rotation,

---

Each individual has a lot of freedom here, yet we also try to check in with each other before doing something we think someone might not like.

---

four to five nights a week. Cobbling together various freelance activities, none of us have regular nine-to-five jobs, so we're around a lot. And we had an awfully nice solstice ceremony last week, just the four of us. Huh. Am i living in community or not?

Well, yes and no. The assumptions here are different. With Walnut St., as with Acorn, it was always our intention that the community would outlast my tenure or that of any other particular resident. This place, in contrast, is completely dependent on Alex's continued

Alex installs more shelves in the kitchen in order to hold all the bulk foods from the food co-op. Piece by piece, the building is converted from housing one person to four.

residency; it doesn't have an identity above and beyond his current ownership of the property. Since the four of us don't have meetings, we obviously haven't gone through the clarifying of common purpose that is strongly recommended by consultants (including me) to forming communities.

Because my three housemates don't have the long experience with alternative culture that i do, i can't presume that our values are the same regarding food choices, transportation, and other lifestyle traits. However, in order to save money, one car has already been sold. Since i'm the main food shopper, i focus on getting the bulk of our food from the local co-op plus a CSA farm. People have been willing to show videos in private rooms rather than the living room, which matters a lot to me. And in some areas, like humanure, others are ahead of me in knowledge or commitment.

Each individual has a lot of freedom here, yet we also try to check in with each other before doing something we think someone might not like. It's basically a much less formal lifestyle than i've been accustomed to. I love the mental space and energy that has been freed up by that, and the lower stress level. On the other hand, i sometimes feel frustrated or confused when things aren't going the way i want and there isn't a clear path to addressing it.

Our backgrounds are different, and we don't all know each other well yet. We have our tensions and awkward moments, results of shifting moods or misunderstandings or simple differences. In those times, i think each of us searches for a combination of internal groundedness and external tolerance. Hmm?... Maybe living here isn't as different as i thought?

After all, it's not like *any* intentional community is filled with people who are exactly alike, or understand each other perfectly. No matter how well-crafted the vision statement, there is always the possibility for different interpretations to arise—and given enough time, they probably will. While people applying for membership always emphasize how well they'll fit in with a community's existing values and how the group likes to run things, from what i've observed most applicants have gaps in honesty or self-awareness (or both) that end up significantly impacting the group later on.

At this household, i don't know whether to say that we have no membership process at all, or that we have a process more extensive than any of the communities i've lived at. What it comes down to is that we want to live with people who we already have an established friendship with, and who our instincts (along with a dose of common sense) tell us are a good match.

While right now our "membership" is limited to the four of us, we've also had another neighbor sharing dinners with us, and several friends who've slept on our floor for days or weeks at a time. Thus the isolation i feared doesn't seem to be coming to pass. We've also been intentional about inviting friends to join us for dinner, recognizing that social interaction isn't as built-in here as it is when a group is on the recognized community circuit.

For me, living in an informal group house of this sort is as much of an experiment as joining a commune might be for someone else. I don't know if this will settle into being a long-term situation for the four of us or not. I strive to remain open-minded and exploratory in my approach. I remember the commitment i made when i left Acorn, to let go of forms, to be open to emergence and the fullness of life's calling.❀

Tree Bressen works as a freelance facilitator and group process skills teacher for intentional communities and other organizations, mainly in the Cascadia bioregion. See www.tree-group.info. (Tree uses a lower-case "i" in her articles as an expression of egalitarian values.)

Author Tree Bressen

Gardens of Gratitude:
A Two-Day Garden Party Blitz in L.A

By Ginny LeRossignol Blades

All photos courtesy of Ginny LeRossignol Blades

Seeds of community, sustainability, and change were sown in a very large and fertile field when the Westside Permaculture Group of Los Angeles launched a two-day gardening blitz last May called **Gardens of Gratitude: Growing Food and Community.**

This grassroots collective, calling themselves The Westside Permies, offered free advice, resources, and labor to anyone willing to plant edibles who signed up on their Gardens of Gratitude website (www. GardensOfGratitude.org). The garden party was a congenial yet subversive celebration of goodwill, inspiring individual gardening confidence and self-reliance while mobilizing neighborhoods toward growing food and sharing their bounty with each other. In all, 96 new gardens sprouted up over the weekend.

No project was too small—or too large—for the Gardens of Gratitude campaign: from tomatoes potted for apartment balconies to full-scale operations where entire front yards or empty lots were converted into bountiful "Victory Gardens."

Each site participant teamed up with a certified master gardener or permaculture consultant "mentor" who donated his or her time for the event. Free or low-cost compost or mulch was available by the truckload, in some cases even delivered on-site by a friendly stranger. Roving teams of volunteer work crews of every skill level helped make it all happen in "barn-raising" party style.

Part of the inspiration of Gardens of Gratitude came from the Victory Gardens of WWII, when in response to food rationing, shortages, and government encouragement, nearly 20 million Americans planted gardens in backyards, empty lots, and even city rooftops. Neighbors pooled their resources, grew different kinds of foods, and formed cooperatives.

Sean Jennings, a spokesperson for the Westside Permies, says the key to pulling off a huge undertaking like Gardens of Gratitude was in having a small, cohesive community of like-minded people assembled around a clear purpose. They hope their example will inspire other groups around the country and world to create similar events to catalyze community and local food sustainability. ✿

Ginny LeRossignol Blades, former COMMUNITIES *Art Director, lives in L.A.*

Chicken à la West Birch Avenue

We used to be a typical neighborhood. People were friendly enough and we waved to each other on our way into and out of our houses. We had the occasional chat on the sidewalk while shoveling snow or doing yard work. But that was where community ended on our block of West Birch Avenue in Flagstaff, Arizona. Our shady, tree-lined, historic downtown neighborhood mirrored countless neighborhoods across the United States: polite, but disconnected.

Knowing how valuable a connected neighborhood is, I had always wanted to create more meaningful neighborhood relationships than just small talk on the sidewalk. For one reason or another it never happened until one day when our neighborhood started a process that enabled us to connect in real ways. It began when my husband Pete and I consulted with a permaculture landscape company that was creating a design for our backyard. When they suggested we get chickens to eat our food scraps, make fertilizer, and provide eggs, I dismissed it immediately, thinking that chickens were far too ambitious for us as a single family with a five-year-old, a baby, and two cats. We had our plates full already.

I mentioned the landscape plan to our neighbor Jessie and suddenly a concept began to germinate: we could create a neighborhood chicken co-op! The idea had brilliant energy and momentum. The project gelled during a neighborhood potluck hosted at our house. We talked with more neighbors (Mark, who is also Pete's brother; his partner Jamie; Jessie's partner Brin; Sara; and Eric). We realized that we had five households of people on our block who were excited about the project. As we sat at our dining room table we discussed our collective ignorance about chickens, our fears about being able to care for them effectively, and our concerns that they would be noisy and smelly.

Despite these obstacles, Jessie decided to join because, in her words, "it was an opportunity to regain a relationship with the food we eat, and in the process a deeper connection to the natural world and our neighbors." Sara was dubious but decided to go along with it because we were proposing housing the chickens in her backyard and she didn't want to stand in the way of the project. For Pete and me, it was an opportunity to give our kids an experience that would highlight our values of sustainable local foods and community. By the end of the potluck, we were all committed.

It took shape quickly. One of the best things about the project was how each neighbor applied his or her unique skills. Jessie was the only one of us who had any experience with chickens, so she volunteered to keep the tiny chicks in her kitchen for their first couple weeks of life. She spearheaded the task of checking the chicks' vents several times each day to ward off pasty butt and keep them healthy. Our daughter Gemma and Eric's daughter Ellie were enamored with the chicks and Jessie left her back door unlocked during the day so the kids could visit them.

Eric had a friend with chickens, so he kindly arranged for us to borrow supplies we would need, like a large tub to house the chicks as they grew. At this stage, the chicks moved to our garage, where Pete used an old door from our basement and some chicken wire to rig up a "roof" to the tub so the chicks would be safe from our cats. Everyone in the neighborhood had the code to open the garage so they could visit the chicks during the day. I loved seeing how effortlessly the boundaries of private space began to open as the neighbors united in this common endeavor.

Mark owns the duplex where Jessie, Brin, and Sara are tenants, and he suggested that we use the old horse barn behind the duplex house for a coop. Pete and Mark developed a design for the coop that would keep our chickens warm in winter, cool in summer, and safe from foxes, skunks, and raccoons. Again, Pete harvested old windows and building supplies from our basement to create the coop. We were all so excited when we located some paint that was being given away free by the city to paint the inside of the coop.

The chicks grew rapidly and Pete, Mark, Eric, and Brin worked diligently on the construction of the coop. When it was time to put netting over the chicken run to protect them from predators, Jamie and Sara helped watch our baby Angus while other neighbors put up the netting. Gemma helped construct and paint a hot pink ramp for the chickens to go in and out. Meanwhile, I hosted another neighborhood potluck so we could enjoy our success and "talk chickens." Eric organized a chicken rotation and each household now cares for the chickens a week at a time. Of course, if anyone ever needs someone to cover their shift, help is easy to find.

In this project, we have gained much more than fertilizer and eggs. We now have a shared commitment to these little beings that brings us together in satisfying ways. The chicken coop has become a sort of neighborhood commons where impromptu gatherings occur as neighbors stop by to drop off their kitchen

Top left: The chicks. Top middle: Pete and Brin working on the coop. Right: Gemma holding a chick. Bottom middle: The chick are starting to get feathers. Bottom left: Jesse adding the finishing touches.

scraps, give the birds fresh water, or brainstorm about how to fix a hole in the fence. It's a great conversation piece when friends and relatives come to visit; we have been able to meet more of each other's extended networks around the coop. The chickens also make us laugh as we watch them peck over old pieces of lettuce, moldy grapes, and pizza crusts.

Pete and Mark both put gates in their fences so we now have a corridor that runs across the back of three houses, linking us together. I like to see how this has increased our daughter's sense of freedom within the neighborhood. She is now free to run back and forth between the yards and I don't worry about her being alone in the front of the house by the street. Sometimes when Eric brings his daughter over (they live across the street) I'll find that the girls have struck up a spontaneous playtime that may focus around the chickens or extend into our house. It has also increased Gemma's ability to have independent relationships with the adults in our neighborhood. I'm glad that our children have this really cool project to do together and with other adults that enables them to feel freer in the world.

Taking care of these birds has created a shared sense of compassion and responsibility. Sara and I have both been surprised at how much we have come to like the chickens in the process of caring for them. One night, a ringtail cat got into the chickens' yard and frightened one bird literally to death. Several of us heard the "ladies" squawking at 5:00 in the morning and Mark came to their rescue. During that day, I noticed how we all shared concern for our birds' safety as we pieced together the details of what happened. Gemma took extra care with the chickens, visiting them often and making them "soup" of weeds and water that she hand-carried to them to help them recover from the scary event.

Another surprise along the way is how easy it was to create a miniature model of sustainable food production in an urban

area. Jessie says, "the chicken co-op has helped me to realize that it's not hard to build community or affect our food system. There isn't any special formula or checklist to follow. A simple potluck is all it takes to bring people together to make a positive change."

I love how this project is also teaching us and our children about the cycles of nature in a tangible way. Daily, we see our kitchen scraps devoured and transformed into poop for our gardens. We are just now starting to get an egg or two each day. For those of us who eat meat, we've had the opportunity to connect to that particular source of food in a real way.

In our neighborhood, we are allowed to have only hens and not roosters due to a city ordinance. So when we discovered that two of our original 16 chickens were roosters, we decided to slaughter and butcher them. This decision was something most of us felt squeamish about—a testament to how disconnected we are from the meat we eat. Most of us did not feel up to the task, but Pete and Eric volunteered and went through the process together from start to finish. Afterward, Pete and I cooked the roosters into broth and stew meat, which is in our freezer. The kids (who were not as squeamish as the adults) later saw pictures and heard the details of how it all happened, creating an important link for them in understanding where meat comes from, and seeing how their care and nurturing can contribute to the food we eat.

The next neighborhood potluck is due in a couple weeks, and we will be enjoying chicken soup à la West Birch Avenue, and perhaps a quiche or an omelet, homestyle. ✳

Hilary Giovale is a mother, writer, and belly-dance instructor in Flagstaff, Arizona. She holds a Master's degree in sustainability from Northern Arizona University.

Lighten Up:

A Community Energy-Reduction Experiment

*By Kelly Barth, with editorial advice and guidance from fellow
Kawsmonauts Deborah Altus, Doug Hitt, Noelle Kurth, and Elizabeth Schultz*

The famed Harvard biologist, E.O. Wilson, has said, "The epic of evolution is the best myth we will ever have." Wilson joins a chorus of voices calling for us to reclaim our story, our 13.7 billion-year-old evolutionary and ecological identity. Spatially and temporally, humans don't end or begin at our skin. We are woven into a vast and ancient web of relationship. We personally and collectively feel the reverberations of all that heals or harms that web.

What if a community of people organized themselves around this unfolding myth? How would they impact their bioregion? How would their own lives be impacted? Six years ago, a group of people, varying in ages and backgrounds, met in a living room in Lawrence, Kansas, to find out. The current gathering of 16 people, which we call Kawsmos (a nod to our local Kansas

or "Kaw" River watershed and the Kaw Nation that once inhabited the area), has organized around three core values.

The first, **New Story Telling**, says we will engage the insights of cosmology and ecology in artful and provocative ways. We study and discuss the teachings of Thomas Berry, Brian Swimme, and Joanna Macy, to name a few. We take field trips. We perform and create eco-rituals. We write and perform science-as-theater, dramatizing key moments in evolutionary history, such as the emergence of photosynthesis. The group explores cosmic and earthly interactions and connections through collaborative painting and embodies them through dance.

Our second value, **Quality of Interaction**, distinguishes conversation from mere discussion. Conversation—literally *being-in-company-with*—honors silence as well as words; it asks

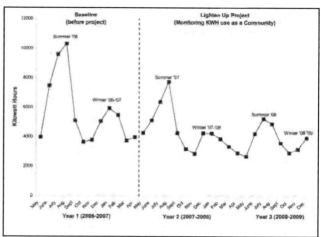

Opposite page: The Kawsmos community after a recent gathering focused on the universe story. Above left: "Lighten Up" display used by the community to track energy usage each month. The display depicts individual maximums, minimums, and means as well as total group usage. The display serves to engage the group in meaningful, concrete discussion and provide motivation for conservation. Each full coal car represents 1000 kWh of group energy usage. Display construction and photo by Tom Mersmann. Above right: This chart depicts total group energy usage in kilowatt hours (kWh) per month over a 2-1/2 year period with seasonal changes noted. From May 2006-April 2007, we were not engaging in any conservation efforts (the data were collected retroactively). From May 2007-December 2008, efforts to lessen energy usage were underway. Data collection and graph by Deborah Altus and Noelle Kurth.

participants to be aware of not only their own internal feelings and thoughts but also those of others who might be more reticent to join the stream. Fundamentally, authentic conversation aims at the mutual discovery of wisdom—both the Earth's and ours. All of us are responsible for creating a safe space for fully inclusive conversation, risk-taking, and play. Practically speaking, a rotating planning group arranges and facilitates our monthly meetings.

Third, we value **Enactment** within the local socio-ecological community. For example, given the urgency of climate change, we decided we could not simply wait until alternative energy infrastructures materialized around us. Our planning committee made the timely suggestion that we reduce our collective carbon footprint. To narrow and focus our efforts, we decided to tackle our electricity usage. The resulting two-year energy reduction and awareness project we called "Lighten Up."

With some initial quakes and flutters, we committed to forwarding our monthly electric usage numbers, for the previous 12 months and each month to follow, to a member excited by tracking these statistics. We agreed this wouldn't be about guilt or competition, unlike the programs of a growing number of utility companies around the country, such as the Sacramento Municipal Utility District. We weren't going, as they did, to draw frowny or smiley faces on each other's monthly utility bill.[1] But we knew changing light bulbs wouldn't be enough. We would need to make some fairly substantial lifestyle changes if we wanted to achieve meaningful reductions. We collectively made this commitment to our bioregion and each other on the cusp of the hothouse swelter of a northeast Kansas summer. Should we lose our nerve, we needed only to look at the long trains of coal daily rumbling to the power plant belching at our city's edge. We needed only to remember a 10-year-old among us who volunteered to read his bedtime books by candlelight.

Some of us knew how difficult this would be. We held our tongues when a menopausal member wondered aloud whether she could survive without air-conditioning. We already knew how asexual, yet creative, everyone would become by high summer.

As expected, we sometimes arrived at meetings haggard and glistening like fellow survivors of a shipwreck. "One of my favorite chairs is molding," one member sighed. Another confessed to succumbing to a wall unit after a string of 100+°F days. Coming home to an un-air-conditioned house after working in an office cold as a refrigerator felt like inviting a heart attack. Everyone tried to stay upbeat. It wasn't bad if you didn't move.

This isn't the kind of experiment you want to undertake alone. For instance everyone had a vested interest in one member's research about airflow. We learned which windows to open depending on sun position and wind strength and direction, when to turn on a window fan and when to leave it off. We found that window fans can be just as effective at cooling a room as a window unit air-conditioner. We all said farewell to another fiercely held myth about air-conditioning when we discovered that even on the hottest days, leaving the A/C on all day consumes more energy than turning it off when you aren't home and turning it on when you return. To our manifest surprise, it doesn't take that long for a warm house to cool down again once you do turn the A/C on. "This whole project makes you think and negotiate," said one couple. "You have to decide when to sleep, where to sleep. I'll admit, we still have arguments about what works best. And when you're hot and sleepy, you don't want to argue. But ultimately, you can deal with it. You just have to be open to changing the way you do things, adjusting blinds, staying quiet in the afternoon." Yes, it was stultifying on some nights, but we all knew that in a few days, it would be bearable again. In fact, pre-meeting potlucks often focused on the weather. Like farmers, we stood in small circles speculating about fronts. We communally rejoiced when they blew in, often purple and green with rain, cooling our skin and breaking our fever.

"We just had to turn on the A/C one week," the most stalwart of members lamented. "The heat we could take but heat with humidity—we thought we might die, really. But then the air felt unnaturally cold, and we missed the night sounds, cicadas, crickets. It was too quiet. We felt isolated. It makes me wonder how many summers I've missed." Everyone agreed that it helps knowing that, all over your town, you have a core group of others sweating, tossing, turning, and being lulled finally to sleep by the same creatures outside your bedroom window.

For some, the experiment had everything to do with the long-lost art of frugality. "I'm an empirical person," said one member. "I don't like giving my money to utilities, so I turn the lights off when I leave a room, and I turn the heat down when I'm away. I retired early, and even though I get a pension, I need to watch my money. I want to live my life so that the quotidian stuff is basic, so that I can save for things I really want to do like take a trip to Machu Picchu." One member is in the process of replacing some of her electric appliances, such as her coffee grinder, can-opener, and hand-drill, with human-powered ones of the past.

Always in the back of everyone's minds were the numbers. We depended on each other to keep these numbers in check. Ethical dilemmas arose. Friends with a new baby showed up on one member's doorstep holding a gargantuan sack of wet diapers and asking to use her long dormant dryer because theirs was on the fritz. She had to think twice. "I sat in the light of an organic-soy-based-made-in-a-100-percent-solar-powered-factory-candle, martyr that I am, and felt the kilowatt hours ticking away." A low point for another couple came when they got their first winter electric bill. "It was really, really bad. We had a new hot tub, but we didn't have it on the economy setting. After all that work, in just one month, we'd blown our savings. It was an "aha!" moment." A wildlife rehabilitator in the group admitted her spring numbers were up because she'd had to leave a heating pad on continually for a group of neonate opossums whose mother had been killed by a car.

One member constructed a three-dimensional display of wooden coal cars stacked on pegs to represent our monthly electricity usage. Visualizing our personal electricity use as actual cars of coal was essential motivation in the face of small discomforts. With each coal car representing 1000 kilowatt hours of group energy usage, we could easily digest our impact.

In the end, consensus was that "Lighten Up" had been far less painful than any of us had imagined. Collectively, we had reduced our consumption by 25 percent. We had survived—thrived even. As we watched Kansas Governor Kathleen Sebelius tenaciously veto bill after bill that would have allowed construction of two 700-megawatt coal-fired power plants in the state, our experiment became all the more meaningful. Kawsmos has moved on to other projects, but we continue to collect and examine our electricity usage and are eager share our experience with others. We grow together as a community, energized by working collectively to reclaim our story. ❈

Freelance writer Kelly Barth and her partner and fellow Kawsmonaut, landscape painter Lisa Grossman, and their two cats live happily on little money in a very small house in Lawrence, Kansas. The two have been a part of the Kawsmos community since 2005—just in time for a year of studying the sun and the resultant "Lighten Up" energy-reduction project. All residents of Douglas County, Kansas, the Kawsmonauts meet monthly in each other's homes for potlucks and interdisciplinary study and celebration of various aspects of their home bioregion, planet, galaxy, and universe.

How the Kawsmonauts Lowered Electric Usage

Here are a few things Kawsmonauts did to lower electric usage:
- Installed attic fans.
- Installed exhaust fans.
- Added awnings.
- Used thermal drapes or blinds.
- Installed programmable thermostats.
- Replaced aging appliances with Energy Star models.
- Used ceiling fans and turned them off when humans or pets weren't in the room, since they cool only living things not air.
- Used a combination of water mister and fans on warm nights.
- Retreated to the basement on summer afternoons.
- Put appliances on power strips and turned them off when nothing was in use.
- Cooked outside during summer (i.e. rice cooker, crock pots).
- Used microwaves, especially in the summer.
- Used pressure cookers, which cook quickly and have the added benefit of not adding heat to the room.
- Switched to compact fluorescent bulbs.
- Hung clothes on indoor/outdoor clotheslines.
- Closed and opened blinds as outdoor temperatures demanded.
- Installed insulated, reflective paper in attic.
- Used weather stripping.
- Used flannel sheets in the winter.
- Used bamboo sheets in the summer.
- Left hot water in the tub after a bath in winter to raise room temperature and humidity.
- Painted houses a light color, since we're in a Southern zone.
- Used solar/crank radios.
- Used analog telephones.

1. Kaufman, Leslie. "Utilities Turn Their Customers Green, With Envy," *New York Times*, January 30, 2009.

What Are the Boundaries of an Intentional Community?

An Experiment in Geographically-Dispersed Community-Building

By Don Schneider and Elin England

Where and How it Began, and How it Went
In a rural community in the beautiful Cascade foothills just outside of Eugene, Oregon, a group of community-minded families joined together for a number of years to talk, share, cooperate, and eat. Elkdream Farm, an eight-acre parcel with good agricultural soils, good sun, and good water, was the primary host-location for what we came to call the Pleasant Hill Progressives—a group of mostly progressive and environmentally-oriented, secular, middle-class, and middle-aged individuals.

Many of the group's members had lived in communal households during college and for a number of years (in some cases decades) afterward. But over time, the pull of the broader culture toward individual pursuits had lured us all toward separate lives. Our family moved to Pleasant Hill just after our second child was born, drawn to the area by the promise of good schools and dreams of establishing a large kitchen garden and orchard. As we got to know the community, we discovered that we were surrounded by a mix of very conservative, old-school rural Oregonians with good hearts and rigid views; wealthy professionals busily buying up old mobile homes and replacing them with McMansions; and an assortment of young and old hippies with more alternative mindsets.

What we did not find, however, were avenues to connect with our fellow Pleasant Hill residents in ways other than attending one of the many churches or involving ourselves with the school sports programs. In an attempt to establish some community for ourselves and find others of a like mind, we instigated a discussion group based on the Northwest Earth Institute's (nwei. org) format. Starting first with Voluntary Simplicity, we went on to explore several other topics in the NWEI series revolving around environmental and social change issues, before launching onto our own path. We found our way through a Peak Oil phase, reading and discussing works by Richard Heinberg, James Howard Kunstler, and other notables of that genre. We also began discussing the question, "What does it mean to be a community?"

It became clear that we were, in some ways, functioning in a conscious, intentional way as a self-declared community. To be sure, we all lived in our own geographically-dispersed homes, none of them on the same tax lot; we had our own separate lives, and paid our own separate bills. We weren't sharing a bathroom and kitchen with each other, one measure of living communally—nor, separated by several miles, could we hope to consider ourselves a cohousing community. But we were, in fact, meeting with some regularity, sharing food, and developing our own culture, customs, and closeness. We were cooperating as an intentional-but-dispersed, rural "virtual" community.

At the peak of our group's membership, 43 people gathered for a summer potluck. But more typically, there were about 12 to 15 at any particular meeting, unless it was a special occasion. We had an email newsletter for a while that helped maintain cohesion among the larger group by reporting what we had discussed at the last meeting, what was on the agenda for the next meeting, what was on the horizon in terms of action items, and any other reminders or follow-up issues. We visited and hosted speakers from other intentional communities in our area. We had a calendar of seasonal events including bonfires, labyrinth walks, coordinated plantings among households for sharing at harvest time, coordinated bulk food purchases from local food producers, food preservation and holiday parties, and even a collective chicken harvest—an educational if somewhat grisly affair.

Because many of us had school-aged children, we were a "kids welcome" community by default. We found that Sunday gatherings at 3 p.m. worked best—discussion from 3 to 5, potluck from 5 to 7. Everyone went home on Sunday evening fed and feeling good with no need to cook dinner and plenty of time to get ready for the work and school week ahead.

We met successfully for several years twice a month from September through June. Summer vacation schedules proved too scattered to make regular meetings feasible during July and August. However, as the kids got older and busier, and as the increasingly frenetic pace of modern-day, middle-class con-

Left: Community campfire at a gathering of the Pleasant Hill Progressives. Right: Summer games.

sumerist lives took its toll, the group began to lose focus and momentum. We began meeting just once a month for what we called our "Second Sunday" gathering. And finally, at our summer break in 2008, we decided to discontinue our regular meetings. Now we mostly just get together informally, often in smaller subgroups, or for special occasions.

What Worked, What Didn't Work, and What We Learned

First, we learned that a sense of community and a feeling of belonging are not limited by geography, and that a positive aspect of having geographical distance between households is that many of the usual communitarian concerns—pets, chores, noise, and so forth—do not become issues. And we reaffirmed our belief that eating together is good, natural, healthy, human behavior and essential to feeling connected and nourished as community.

However, we also learned that it is hard to maintain momentum and move forward in a coordinated manner when you don't live within walking distance of each other. Maintaining community cohesion seems harder in a rural area than in an urban or suburban neighborhood, because you don't cross paths or see each other on the street coming-and-going as often—you have to get in a car and drive several miles after a long day. Ugh!

We also learned that it is hard to keep motivation, commitment, and leadership going unless people really grasp the concept of what it means to be a self-organizing group. *Everyone* has to take responsibility for making the group happen, or it will fizzle out. In the early stages of the group, meetings were held at various members' houses on a rotating basis. Although this was difficult when families with children came to meetings at homes that were not childproofed, it did facilitate more of a shared sense of responsibility for the group by those serving as the host.

Connected with this, we found that while some people have issues with structure and leadership, in fact, having some structure is helpful—it brings continuity, coherence, and meaning to

time spent together. When there is a predictable schedule that can be planned around, a set number of meetings so there is an end in sight, a specified ending time that is respected, and tasks assigned in between meetings having to do with specific topics or agenda items, then cohesion and satisfaction are strengthened and people are more willing to make time in their busy schedules for the group. This was evidenced in the early stages of the group, when we were utilizing the structure provided by the eight-week Northwest Earth Institute discussion courses. The expectations were clear, the beginning and end points were clear, and structure was provided, even if we strayed from it at times. The group seemed to flow very well, and meetings were well attended. In contrast, when we moved away from NWEI, guidelines and expectations were hazy, and participation dropped off.

In addition, in our desire to be egalitarian about steering the direction of the group, we also suffered from a lack of leadership, particularly after we moved away from using the NWEI courses. As a result, the aim or purpose of the group, other than coming together as community, was not always clear. Without more leadership and structure to mobilize the potential of the group for satisfying and effective action, the focus faded and people began to drift away. We were not, it seems, able effectively to move the group focus from being a social gathering back to having a greater purpose, despite our attempts to encourage the group to engage in self-reflection and refocus.

We knew that working toward emotional closeness and strong relationships is essential to realizing our vision of a better world, but we were unable, except on rare occasions, to provide an effective context conducive to talking about deeper emotions. As a result, on the occasions when discussion turned, for instance, to deeper feelings of concern about the state of the world (e.g., despair, frustration, fear, etc.), these expressions were too often met with a somewhat cynical, joking attitude, or other interjections which tended to derail the discussion and prevented deeper exploration that might have led the group to a stronger level of commitment. We also lacked a specific, agreed-upon process or method for resolving conflicts. These factors, along with the natural pull to socialize and seek pleasure rather than explore and possibly experience discomfort, led, over time, to stagnation and kept the group from evolving. Our collectively conditioned middle-class tendencies to keep things pleasant conflicted with the possibility of greater depth and closeness. The cultural tendency toward individualism prevailed over the ideal of communitarian pursuits. People drifted off and the group disbanded.

We began the group with a rather relaxed attitude of "Come if you want, hope you can make it," without requiring any sort of commitment. And out of a desire to be inclusive, we had a policy of "taking all comers" without any sort of pre-screening or criteria for inclusion. These were errors and proved to be detrimental to group cohesion and progress in numerous ways. The constant churning of new faces resulted in frequently having to go back to square one in terms of information that had been presented. Not being more selective resulted in some amount of interpersonal discomfort that kept interactions at a more superficial social level and was disruptive to the formation of a solid, committed core group. Comments from established members such as "I'm sorry, but I'm never coming again if that person is going to be part of this group" revealed just how important the screening process is.

So What's Next?

We are still interested in cooperative community and cooperative economics. There is still interest among several of the past members in building a community group with more commitment, depth, and focus that is outcome-oriented. What that will look like is, as yet, undetermined. But we are very clear about the importance that community has in our lives. ✤

Don Schneider and Elin England have been together through several life-chapters over the last 27 years. They hosted the Pleasant Hill Progressives at their home, Elkdream Farm, in western Oregon for eight years. They are currently looking into prospects for developing a senior-friendly (though not exclusively elder) cohousing community in the south Willamette valley of Oregon. They can be contacted at elkdream_farm@yahoo.com.

Eating Close to Home

Eating Close to Home: A Guide to Local Seasonal Sustenance in the Pacific Northwest *by Elin Kristina England. 2009, 232 pages. ISBN 978-0-578-00069-5. elkdream_farm@yahoo.com.*

The author collected recipes from her own kitchen and from gardeners, farmers, and food-lovers in her local community (including some of the Pleasant Hill Progressives) to create a bioregional, seasonal cookbook intended to help Pacific Northwesterners eat close to home year-round. Sections take readers through Winter, Spring, Summer, and Fall, describing both familiar and almost-forgotten vegetables and fruits and how to prepare them into delicious "nibbles," salads, soups, main dishes, side dishes, baked goods, and tasty treats. Additional chapters contain dishes that fit any season, instructions on putting food by, and resources for going more local. The following are excerpted from a list of helpful websites on pp. 220-221:

The 100 Mile Diet. **100milediet.org**. A website started by Alisa Smith and J.B. MacKinnon, authors of *Plenty*, the book detailing their year of eating only what food could be obtained within a 100 mile radius of their home in Vancouver, BC. The website has stories from people all over the world interested in eating locally, lots of suggestions for how to make your diet more sustainable, and a mapping tool to help you figure out the parameters of your local foodshed.

Chef's Collaborative. **chefscollaborative.org**. A national network of chefs, food producers, educators, and food lovers who come together to celebrate local foods and foster a more sustainable food supply. On their site you can find restaurants all over the country that serve locally grown foods.

Eat Local. **www.eatlocal.net**. An extremely informative, easy-to-use website with links to many great resources across the US. It also has lots of great recipes, inspiring articles, and lots of support for those who want to make their diet more sustainable.

Eat Well Guide. **www.eatwellguide.org**. A guide for finding fresh, wholesome, sustainable food in the US and Canada. The site lists farms, stores, restaurants, and outlets.

Edible Communities. **www.ediblecommunities.com**. Their mission is to transform the way communities shop for, cook, eat, and relate to the food that is grown and produced. Through printed publications, websites, and events, they connect consumers, from a variety of regions across the country, with local growers, retailers, chefs, and food artisans, enabling those relationships to grow and thrive in a mutually beneficial, healthful, and economically viable way.

Urban Edibles. **urbanedibles.org**. An intriguing site created by a cooperative network of wild food foragers. Based in Portland [Oregon], their ideas could well be expanded to include other areas. The site includes a map of where in Portland one can find various wild edibles, plus information on identifying and harvesting edible and medicinal plants, preservation techniques, and other useful tidbits.

Greening Your 'Hood

An ignorant kid from the suburbs learns the lessons of living sustainably—from kibbutzes to ecovillages, from cohousing to pocket neighborhoods

By David Leach

When I was 20, I ran away from home to live on a kibbutz in northern Israel. I wasn't Jewish. I wasn't Marxist. I wasn't a back-to-the-lander. I wasn't even seeking (in the words of one volunteer coordinator) the "sun, sand, and sex" that has drawn 350,000 young visitors to the 270-plus communal villages of Israel's famous kibbutz movement.

No, I was escaping both a broken heart and the claustrophobia of growing up in the most middle-class neighborhood, in the most middle-class city, in the most middle-class country in the world. (Ottawa, Canada, if you must know.) I landed by chance on Kibbutz Shamir, near the border with Syria, which had been founded in 1944 by hardcore Romanian socialists.

As a new volunteer, I learned that the kibbutz movement embodied the "purest form of communism in the Western world." (Fifteen years later, kibbutz members would ditch Marxism, privatize Shamir, and list its optical factory on the NASDAQ stock exchange.) I was less impressed by the radical ideals of the kibbutz, however, than its architecture and design. I had grown up in a subdivision where the car was king. Like almost every suburb since Levittown, New York, my neighborhood had been designed to move vehicles quickly from A to B, with walkers and cyclists considered a nuisance or an after-thought. Commercial activity and social hubs had been zoned far from its long crescents of setback homes and double garages. (In fact, the only store you could reach by foot was an automotive dealership.) Cemented into this suburban DNA was an Orwellian message: Two cars, good; two legs, bad.

On the kibbutz, I discovered the simple joy of life on a human scale at a human pace. Like most kibbutzes, Shamir had been purpose-built in concentric circles of small buildings and row houses, linked by pedestrian pathways. A multi-purpose dining hall and an open green space exerted a centripetal force to draw everyone into the community's center. No resident lived more than a 10-minute amble from this hub, where they could share meals, debate issues, and celebrate holidays together.

We wandered down car-free paths to our workplaces every morning, and later to the general store, the bar, the library, the sports hall (which doubled Tuesday nights as a movie theatre), and the swimming pool. These informal gathering sites acted like "third places"—the phrase that American sociologist Ray Oldenburg coined for the casual in-between spaces (like cafés and hair salons, neither work nor home) so vital to a truly democratic society.

On the kibbutz, cars were few, shared among members, and sequestered in peripheral parking lots. Walking formed the fabric of everyday life. So, too, did the conversations sparked by unexpected footpath encounters. Who needed Facebook—still 15 years away—when you could collect the daily news by strolling to the kitchen for an after-dinner snack?

In a quirk of etymology, *kibbutz* (Hebrew for "gathering") and *kibitz* (Yiddish for "chitchat") sound remarkably similar. That confusion contains an accidental truth: At the heart of any community

Kibbutz Degania.

Street party in Victoria.

Neighbor harvesting produce with author's son.

beats the power of positive gossip, the semi-random conversations that bind friends and neighbors together. That was why the early kibbutzniks built their communities to promote kibitzing.

• • •

Communal life changed me, of course, as it does most people. But the transformation wasn't instantaneous, like a flash from the heavens. I didn't return home to found a commune or live in a co-op. I didn't even join a neighborhood association. No, for the next decade or so, I cut my roots short. Almost every year, I moved (between countries or cities or apartments) for school or work or wanderlust.

Wherever I dropped my backpack, I became conscious of how architecture brings people together or keeps us apart—and how that sense of community impacts the environment, too. I'd grown up in a sprawling Wonder Bread subdivision with the carbon footprint of Godzilla. I later worked for Greenpeace, and my late-blooming ecological awareness nagged at my imagination. Wasn't there a better way to live? Could we design a community to be friendly both to its neighbors *and* to its environment? Could we replicate such eco-'hoods on a large scale, as we'd done with suburbia?

I stumbled across clues to this puzzle in surprising places. My wife and I bought a house in Toronto, Canada's biggest city. It was situated in an odd parallelogram of older duplexes, hemmed in by two busy roads, a subway yard, and a train track. Eco-paradise it was not.

And yet neighbors had turned the geographical constraints to their advantage. They had christened this forgotten corner "The Pocket"—a micro-neighborhood that didn't exist on any official map. One family opened their doors every Saturday to sell fresh-baked bread. Other residents published a regular newsletter to broadcast the history, culture, personalities, and urgent issues of The Pocket. (It evolved into a lively online social network.) A sense of community developed around what had been just another postal code. This common purpose was built, like the kibbutz movement, on a foundation of shared myth. We weren't isolated strangers, powerless and alone; we were the people of The Pocket.

The Pocket felt like an oasis amid the surrounding megalopolis. Eventually, even this micro-neighborhood couldn't keep my family in a city that was losing its battle with Carmageddon: the endless, angry storms of traffic, the summer "smog days"

when simply breathing seared our lungs. A new job and new dreams carried us west. On the Pacific coast, in Victoria, British Columbia, my wife and I moved into a small bungalow on a cul de sac. We could have afforded something bigger and newer on the edge of the city. But we liked the proximity of our new home. It was on a bus route and walking distance to a village-like main street of small shops, two grocery stores, a library, recreation center, a dozen cafes and restaurants, and several schools. We wouldn't need to buy a car right away. (Eight years later, thanks to a car-share co-op, we still haven't.)

Oddly, the house's backyard had a hot tub but no side fence. (Perhaps the old owner was an exhibitionist.) It was assumed we would keep the jacuzzi and erect a fence for privacy. We did the opposite: got rid of the energy-hogging tub and left the yard open.

A funny thing happened: We got to know our neighbors. We didn't need to strain over a fence to chat. When my son was born, he began crawling across the invisible property line and into their strawberry patch. Soon, our neighbor took him under her wing, gave him seedlings, and helped him plant a patch of his own. Over the years, she has become his garden mentor and "shirttail aunt"—closer to him than many of his blood relations. He brings her our old newspapers; she teaches him Spanish and how to prune berry bushes. We look after their house when they're away; they let us borrow their car to run errands. That casual sharing might never have happened had a fence stood between us.

• • •

As I learned to accept the kindness of neighbors, I became aware of a global movement that was taking greater steps toward sustainable living. Soon phrases like "ecovillage" and "cohousing" no longer seemed alien to my ears. (O.U.R. Eco-village, on Vancouver Island, had sprung up not far from where I lived.) I visited a few communities and talked to experts to glean lessons from these new pioneers.

Last fall, I met Charles Durrett, the guru of the North American cohousing movement, when he came north to advise two ecovillages on the mainland of British Columbia. "The most successful ecovillages," he told me, "have cohousing as part of them." On an earlier visit, he had asked residents to face each other in two rows, so they could calculate the ideal distance between their future homes. The car-free commons that would separate their porches had to be wide enough for privacy and yet near enough so they could gauge, at a glance, whether a neighbor needed a joke or a hug or to be left alone.

That weekend, Durrett was helping ecovillagers to plan a common house that, like a kibbutz dining hall, would provide a modern, multi-purpose hub of food and friendship and communal activity. He made living ecologically sound *fun* by insisting that residents don't sweat the details, so they could "enjoy a homebrew on the patio together" sooner rather than later. During a break, he spotted a two-story private house across the street, looming on a huge swath of lawn, with an airport runway for its many vehicles.

"You couldn't build a house with a bigger carbon footprint if you tried!" he marveled. (I blushed: it looked like my childhood home.) "Cooking one big pot of spaghetti is more ecological than cooking 30 pots," continued Durrett. "Where I live, we have 34 houses and one lawnmower." That was the simple arithmetic of sustainable sharing at the heart of his cohousing ethic.

Recently, I read a new book by American architect and community planner Ross Chapin, called *Pocket Neighborhoods: Creating Small-Scale Community in a Large-Scale World*. He emphasizes five architectural features that connect neighbors: a central grassy commons or courtyard; a common building, for meetings and shared meals; smaller homes that don't dominate sightlines; low or no fences; and cars kept to the margins. These "pocket neighborhoods" (Chapin has designed several in the Pacific Northwest) can take many forms, from purpose-built ecovillages, to co-op apartments circling a courtyard, to suburban streets in which neighbors have torn down backyard fences or retrofitted rear lanes to create common gathering spaces. They all rely on what Chapin calls a "web of walkability" to get people out of cars and into casual conversations.

From such kibitzing comes cooperation and a truly sustainable sense of community. I began to think of this effect as a neighborhood's K.Q, or "Kibitz Quotient": the social health of any place, judged by the random conversations you have walking through it.

• • •

I still marvel at the *chutzpah* of pioneers I've met, in Israel and elsewhere, who have sacrificed so much to build a better society from scratch. Whether they are octogenarian kibbutz founders or idealistic young ecovillagers, they've shown more vision and courage than I could ever muster.

But I realize that maybe I don't need to sell my house, flee the city again, and live off the grid to save the planet. I belong to the 99 Percent—the vast majority who make our homes in communities more conventional than a commune, an ecovillage, or cohousing. (You can take the kid out of the suburb, I suppose, but you can't take the suburb out of the kid—not all of it, at least.)

And yet many of us 99 Percenters aspire to live more intentionally, too. With a little inspiration, we can all create our own pocket eco-'hoods by reclaiming our yards, our streets, even our suburbs—*from* the cars, *for* the people. We can weave new webs of walkability and rediscover the power of positive gossip to bind a community together. We can tap into the ecological benefits of simple neighborly sharing. We can broadcast our values through hyper-local newspapers and niche social networks to create new myths, rooted in a rich sense of place, so that we all can feel, whatever we're doing—planting a garden, lending a hand, telling a joke—that we're working toward a common good.

We might not build utopia overnight. But we can move toward a greener future, one less fence and one more story at a time. ❧

David Leach is an associate professor of writing at the University of Victoria and a former fellow at the Centre for Cooperative and Community-Based Economy. He is finishing a book about his kibbutz experiences, called Look Back to Galilee: Searching for Utopia in a Divided Land.

O.U.R. Ecovillage.

Natural building is important to residents and students at Tryon Life Community Farm/Cedar Moon community.

LET'S DO GREYWATER FIRST!

COULD THE CITY OF PORTLAND BECOME . . . ECOTOPIA?

Last May, Brenna Bell, president of the board of our nonprofit project, Tryon Life Community Farm (TLC Farm), ran into Portland, Oregon, City Commissioner Sam Adams after his evening keynote address at the annual Village Building Convergence.

Commissioner Adams, as well as other city officials such as Mayor Tom Potter and Commissioner Dan Saltzman, knew all about our project because our "Save the Farm" campaign had recently been on the news so much. The story began four years ago, when an informal network of residents and friends recognized that the seven-acre rented property inside Portland city limits was in dire threat of development. We formed an intentional community (now called Cedar Moon, with 18 adult and five child members) and launched a sustainability education center (TLC Farm) to co-manage the land. *(See "A Farm Grows in Portland, #129, Winter, 2005.)* We have hosted thousands of visitors every year, who learn about everything

The community hopes that the city of Portland will cover alternative, low-tech utilities like this outdoor shower in their regulations.

from earthen plasters to food fermentation and spiritual ecology. We were already playing an important role in Portland's emerging Earth culture as an accessible venue for dialogue and change, and as a place to experiment with stacking diverse land uses to create a more ecologically dense network of creativity. TLC Farm gives people a taste

In our year-long "Save the Farm" campaign we succeeded, but just barely in the nick of time. After solid months of outreach and relationship-building, the last 10 days—during which we had to get approval for $400,000 in uncertain government funding, finalize $600,000 in unapproved bank loans, and raise $150,000 more in general donations from

We're going for "sustainability reform" across Portland's building codes, health codes, and zoning regulations.

of how a new world is possible, arising from the compost of the industrial and capitalist structures. Surrounded by the 650 forested acres of Tryon Creek State Park, we've been creating a new urban ecological paradigm of city-as-forest.

But we weren't going to be able to continue doing this unless we purchased these beautiful woods and meadows—for $1.6 million! If we didn't buy the property by the owner's deadline of January 10, 2006, it was to be sold to a developer who planned to subdivide and build twenty-three luxury mini-mansions!

thousands of supporters—made for an astonishing sprint that captured the attention and imagination of all the major local newspapers, TV stations, politicians, neighbors, and even right-wing shock-jocks. It was a miraculous story—one that transformed the standard image of an inexorable juggernaut of "development" that ravishes all that is healthy in the world, and instead gave us all the opportunity to see ourselves as collaboratively choosing a different future.

But what Commissioner Adams didn't know about when he talked with Brenna was our idea for ReCode Portland, a

Tryon Life Community Farm/Cedar Moon wants alternatives like this earthen building (left) and rocket stove-warmed cob bench (right) to also be covered by local regulations.

campaign to introduce sustainability-oriented regulatory reform across the spectrum of Portland's building codes, health codes, and zoning regulations. So Brenna told him about it. She explained that because our land is zoned residential we would need to get a conditional use permit to continue conducting public programs and educational activities onsite. This is designed to assure the city that our programs wouldn't disrupt the neighborhood or overtax city services—but it would be hugely expensive and take a tremendous amount of time and energy, and might not succeed, given bureau-

also promised both the Park and our neighbors that we won't create parking problems for them.

From our perspective, these challenges simply represent an opportunity to demonstrate the value and effectiveness of alternative approaches to human waste, transportation, and privacy. But the approaches we know can work—site-built composting toilets, greywater management, systematic car-sharing and bicycling, and so on—are either not covered by Portland's current accepted guidelines or might be outright illegal. ReCode Portland is an opportunity for TLC

Clustered and common-wall buildings would be encouraged to preserve open space.

cratic obstacles to the sustainable practices we advocate. For example, our site currently uses pre-existing septic tanks and leach fields. Securing a conditional use permit or starting major new construction the conventional way would require connecting to the city sewer system, which in our case would cost hundreds of thousands more. Moreover, we anticipate bringing many more people to the land to live and to visit as a model of sustainable urban density, and we've

Farm to support the sustainability movement as a place to educate ourselves and each other, to experience a new world as accessible and desirable, and to emerge as empowered agents of change. We don't want to change codes and regulations just for ourselves, but for all sustainable projects in Portland. Many intentional communities choose to "fly under the radar" and build their natural buildings, composting toilets, constructed wetlands, and other sustainable systems in secret, without benefit of local government permission (and be vulnerable to possible fines and shut-downs). We not only didn't want to do that, we *couldn't* do that—our project is far too public. We see this as a timely opportunity to galvanize other people and organizations in the movement to, well . . . legalize sustainability.

To this end, we interviewed a variety of activists and professionals in the natural building movement and developed a list of changes that will not only allow but encourage Earth-cultured human living. These changes encourage structural integrity and reduced toxicity in buildings, local foodshed security, clean water, and deep, mutually beneficial interactions between human and non-human inhabitants.

The new land-use regulations would specifically encourage over-

Residents and students building a light clay-straw composting toilet.

BONSAI MATT JAMES

Volunteers of all ages help with building projects, including this cob sauna and light clay-straw composting toilet.

lapping uses. Residential, commercial, light industrial, educational, agricultural, ecological, and other functions could share the same or adjacent places and built environments, which would save resources, stimulate beneficial relationships, and reduce travel distances and social isolation. New zoning regulations would reduce or eliminate dependency on private vehicles and encourage alternative transportation. Clustered and common-wall buildings would be encouraged to preserve open space. Legal structures would promote

Our next steps will be to convene design charrettes with diverse stakeholders to write well-defined guidelines, codes, and regulations. We will also be pursuing the site-specific conditional use Master Plan required by the City, in which we detail how TLC Farm and Cedar Moon will handle human waste and make the property accessible without driving. We think ReCode Portland has a good chance of succeeding, given the increasing awareness of environmental issues in Portland (even a new "Sustainability Coordinator" position

---

Legal structures would promote shared property-use among small neighborhood clusters.

---

shared property-use among small neighborhood clusters. Wholly new zoning designations could be created: for example, "ecovillage zones." *(See "When 'No' is Just an Uneducated 'Yes'," pg. 39.)*

New building codes would provide simple, usable guidelines for experimental-class and owner-builder-class structures, and for many different kinds of natural buildings and alternative construction: strawbale, woodchip-clay, light straw-clay, earth-bermed homes, temporary structures, non-poured foundations, passive ventilation systems, semi-permeable pavement. New regulations would encourage builders to incorporate thermal mass in their buildings and promote the relatively higher seismic safety of earthen walls. New codes for appropriate technologies would support greywater systems, onsite blackwater treatment, site-built composting toilets, onsite biogas production, as well as masonry stoves and rocket stoves.

has just been created in the Bureau of Development Services). The atmosphere is ripe for continued change.

So, when Brenna told Commissioner Adams our hopes and dreams for ReCode Portland, it was an amazing moment. For most people, in most cities, it's rather intimidating to tell a city official that you're, um, out to change all the rules he or she represents! How would he react?

"You're right," Sam Adams said. "Let's do greywater first!"✿

Laura Dvorak, a recent graduate of Portland International Initiative for Leadership in Ecology, Culture, and Learning program at Portland State University, completed a Master's project on the spiritual aspects of Ecological Sanitation. She has been a core volunteer at TLC Farm for over two years. j. brush is a facilitator, organizer, speaker, financial consultant, and point person for the social ecology working group at TLC Farm. Tryon Life Community Farm: www.tryonfarm.org/share.

Made in the USA
San Bernardino, CA
09 April 2015